MY
TRAVELS
WITH THE BIG C

• and a CLINICAL TRIAL that CHANGED my LIFE •

P.C. PILLETTE-JOHNSON

MY TRAVELS with the BIG C...
and a CLINICAL TRIAL that CHANGED my LIFE

ISBN: 978-1-7360358-0-1 (sc)
ISBN: 978-1-7360358-1-8 (ebk)

pcpillette-johnson.com

CONTENTS

LESSONS

INTRODUCTION

I'M NOT FAMOUS OR INFAMOUS. I haven't travelled the world or lived in a foreign land. I haven't dined with world leaders, made millions in the stock market, nor am I among the young and beautiful. My uniqueness lies in the ability to face cancer and get on with living. Those of us who know The Big C well, quietly go through life doing our thing and getting to the heart of what really matters. We are often short on time so we may seem in a hurry, but don't let that fool you. We're savoring every hour, every minute, every second of every day.

Gardening, walking, reading, and playing tennis are some of my favorite past times, but none more important to me than spending time with my grandkids, Sydney and Aiden. Someone once said that we love our children, but are **in love** with our grandchildren; that fits me to a tee.

At 70 years, I suppose people see me as on the downhill side of life. Strangely, I don't see myself that way. To me oldness is reserved for the infirm and grannies who've had their drivers' licenses revoked by the DMV. I still move pretty good on a tennis court, can walk 2 miles at a healthy clip and even manage on occasion to run after Syd who is 11 and Aiden who is 8. Of course I never catch them, but I've been close a couple times during some serious 'Monkey in the Middle' games. True, parts of me show wear and tear yet I like to see myself as aging well, like a firm block of Tillamook cheese or a fine bottle of Honeywood wine. My mind is sharp and my desire to share what life has taught me is strong.

Writing is another of my very favorite past times, although I've always had a love/hate relationship with its process. It's REALLY hard to find the right words to say exactly what I want to say and it takes great discipline keeping up the search. Margaret Mitchell, author of GONE with the WIND, once stated, "In a weak moment I decided to write a book." I understand her meaning well. I've never been published, yet that hasn't deterred me from trying. With 4 previous books under my belt and their pages yellowing with rejection, I longed to give it one more shot. Democrat Elizabeth Warren and I are a lot alike; we're both from the school of persistence. A major difference between her and me...I have leukemia and she doesn't.

Chronic Lymphocytic Leukemia is a disease of the blood; I have it and there's no cure. Lymphocytes are white blood cells and they work hard to help fight all sorts of infections and keep our immune systems strong. That is, when the cells are normal and healthy. Unfortunately, white blood cells have the capacity to change and become abnormal and unhealthy, crowding out the good ones in a person's blood stream and doing the same in other parts of the human body. Healthy lymphocytes die off on their own and the body produces more of them, but unhealthy ones never die, their numbers just keep going up and up. It's this immortality that can take a person's life.

After years of requiring nothing but regular blood tests to monitor my condition, my WBC (white blood cell count) was at a critically high level and sadly my CLL "watchful waiting" period came to an end. I was faced with the dilemma of going with tried and true treatments or attempting something new. Not the kind of baby boomer to run scared from a challenge, but also a boomer who's kept her old Jitterbug Smartphone over getting a brand new Samsung, I was in a pickle. "To trial, or not to trial; that was the question."

Now let's be honest, trials are a scary thing and often fraught with danger. But we shouldn't despair, because like everything in life, there's always another side. The good news is a clinical trial can also put a person in remission and move back the expiration date we all dread. In my case, its success has given me more time to watch my grandkids grow up, appreciate the important things in life and write a book that just might help people who are wondering whether or not to chance a trial.

Countless books are on the market about clinical trials dealing with the Big C. Unfortunately, most are written by hematologists, research scientists, oncologists; you name it; anything ending in "ists." What people really want and need though, are books written by patients who are seasoned travelers down the road of whatever disease the recently diagnosed must endure. A doctor's explanation, an article on the internet, even an exciting YouTube video never helped me get through 2 bone marrow biopsies, but talking with a friend who'd had 3, did.

I hit gold when Dr. Jeffrey Sharman at the Willamette Valley Cancer Institute and Research Center in Eugene, Oregon, approved me for his Phase II, Bendamustine/Gazyva Chronic Lymphocytic Leukemia Clinical Trial. The good doctor is a noted expert in CLL, as well as medical director of hematology research for *The US Oncology Network*. And by the way, it doesn't hurt that he's easy on the eyes and writes a great CLL blog. Yes, in the little old city of Eugene, home of long distance Olympian Steve Prefontaine and the birthplace of Nike, lives the man who killed the lymphocytes who wanted nothing more than to kill me.

The pre-assessment tests were no piece of cake and the 15 days of Benda and Gazyva infusions were grueling at times with side-effects I wouldn't even wish upon my worst enemy. But the results have been miraculous; lymphocyte counts normal, spleen back to fist size instead of football, energy level up to play competitive tennis with my favorite partner, Donna, and blood full of neutrophils to fight infection. Grateful and happy, you bet I am, but these feelings are tempered by the reality that my blood will eventually turn on me again and I'll start to feel like shit.

Faced with this unique kind of leukemia and traveling through a rigorous clinical trial has taught me a lot about myself and the world around me. I hope my travels and the sharing of 5 simple lessons will help you better live the life you have always wanted.

THE BEGINNING

Like many people with Chronic Lymphocytic Leukemia (CLL), I too was first diagnosed during a routine blood test as part of my yearly physical. Having found out I had breast cancer in 1997, and that diagnosis resulting in a double mastectomy, I was extra vigilant to have check-ups each summer before the start of teaching at South Salem High School in September. My physical exams showed no abnormalities and results of regular blood tests always fell within the standard range. Nothing was ever "flagged" as a concern.

Unfortunately, things were about to change though. It was a Wednesday afternoon in July of 2009, when a nurse from Kaiser Permanente called to tell me my internist had put in orders for a repeat of Monday's blood draw. She added it had something to do with my white blood cell count and CBC with automated differential. Before I had a chance to question what all that meant, she quickened her delivery and added that the lab on Lancaster Drive in Salem was awaiting my arrival, as was the Imaging Department at the same location. For some reason a chest X-ray had also been ordered. I again tried to find out more information, asking this messenger of bad tidings what all these tests were about and what they'd show. She skillfully dodged my questions and in a reassuring voice said this was standard procedure in cases like mine and that my doctor would call me as soon as he got the results. I probed her no further, deciding instead to interrogate my computer.

With the July afternoon suddenly feeling cold and clouded, I went to kp.org, logged in and found blood work that had just been posted. There, in black and white, was my white blood cell value, 23.5. This number had an "H" beside it. Scanning to the right of that letter of the alphabet, the standard range declared, 4.0-10.5. "Damn!" No wonder I was getting a call from my doctor's office. My white blood cell count was over 2 times the top of the normal range. Next, hoping not to find what I was looking for, I read that my lymphocyte numbers were 16.43. This number also had an "H" beside it, and the standard range stared back at me, 1.00-4.80. A muffled, "Mother Fucker" escaped my dry lips as my heart raced.

Leaving the computer, I made a hasty retreat from my home in the suburbs of Keizer, Oregon, to Kaiser Permanente on the crowded 4 lane speedway of Lancaster Drive, about 6 miles away. There was no time to waste; I drove like a bat out of hell. Not knowing what was wrong with me gripped my chest like a vise.

Once in the building, I hurried to the lab area and pulled a number from the little machine that called people to be needled. Seventeen was written on the tiny slip of paper, my lucky number! I figured this was a good sign. Maybe, just maybe, those blood results WERE wrong and my drive down Lancaster's race track was all for naught. After all, my lucky number was 17, wasn't it?

As a robotic voice called out 3 and then 4 and those numbers appeared on the reader board, I realized I was in for a wait. Good hydration always helps phlebotomist's in their search for a decent vein, so I had no problem downing half a bottle of Smart Water. All draws were taken from my left arm or hand because of lymph node dissection in my RIGHT armpit region during the mastectomies. "Increased chance of infection or formation of a blood clot from a right side draw because of diminished lymph node effectiveness," was many a doctor's warning. Sticking to left side pokes was a small price to pay to be a breast cancer survivor, but I could tell some blood drawers weren't always happy to have just one arm to attack.

Seventeen appeared on the board and a tired looking young woman

in a starched white coat guided me to a chair in the lab. I held out my
left arm and she tied a slim band of rubber above my elbow and instructed me to pump a tiny red ball in my palm. I requested a small
needle called a "butterfly" for the draw, and she agreed after a long
search for a good spot to poke. Lucky number 17 proved itself and on
the first try the blood started flowing into a large tube and then drain-
ing into the first of 5 vials labeled with my name and date of birth. I was
on my way to a second blood panel in less than a week. Next, I quickened over to the Imaging Department and again played the numbers
before being called.

Once home, I returned to my computer this time searching sites
like the Mayo Clinic, Johns Hopkins, and MD Anderson to teach me
the truth about higher than normal white blood cells and lymphocytes.
I learned that white blood cells are of 5 major types: neutrophils, lymphocytes, monocytes, eosinophils, and basophils, and each type of cell
plays a different role in protecting the body. The numbers of each one
of these types of white blood cells give important information about
the body's immune system. If a person's individual white blood cell
counts are off, the immune system is compromised. My blood abnormalities, if correct, could mean a variety of conditions, with the most
serious being, leukemia. My sources agreed on that, but with the dog-
gedness of Mr. Monk and Sherlock Holmes, I researched further. No
"alternative facts" or "truthful hyperbole" for me!

Hours later, I'd perused the sites of the American Cancer Society,
National Institute of Health, Lymphoma and Leukemia Society, and
Cancer Centers of America; all said the same thing. The likelihood was
I had some form of leukemia.

The weekend went by with lots of ups and downs. Part of me felt I'd
already paid my dues to fate, destiny, some mighty spiritual power, or
whatever governs one's existence. My beautiful breasts had been given
over to the knife, cut from my chest and sliced into pieces for patho-
logical study and then thrown away. Wasn't that enough in a single
lifetime? Surely another cancer would be more than my fair share to
endure. Then the more rational side took over and I knew that life isn't

fair, tests seldom lie and it was completely possible that something was very wrong with me, again.

I tried hard to stay busy on Saturday and Sunday, doing things I normally did, like get my walk in, play a little tennis, work in the yard and read from a book I'd downloaded on my Kindle. I was in the middle of a great read, THE GIRL WHO SANG to the BUFFALO by Kent Nerburn. Reading became a problem though because being physically still allowed my mind to more easily wander off track from the story and partner up with fear. Another problem was my sweet and loving husband, John. He knew something was off with me and he made that clear with his repeated, "Are you sure you're alright? Are you really sure you're alright?"

My hubby could always spot my attempts at cover ups, probably because we've been together over 30 years. We met in 1986 through a Friendship Ad in the STATESMAN/JOURNAL. This was way before dating sites like Match.com, Zoosk, and eHarmony ever existed, and one reason my lucky number is 17 is because we talked for the first time on the 17th of January.

We checked one another out over the phone before ever agreeing to meet, especially since I hadn't been divorced that long and I had a young daughter. I clearly remember John's ad beginning with, "Need a friend?" Then he followed up with, "26 year old male interested in a female, age 21-40. I like tennis and old movies." The whole ad was music to my ears. Here was a guy who wouldn't be turned off to the fact that I was born in 1948 to his 1958. Besides that, he was someone who wanted a real friend, and he liked two of my favorite things in the whole world. We talked for a long time during our first phone call, and I found out he worked at an elementary school in south Salem and he liked kids, a lot. That was a huge plus for me as a mother.

I've always believed the true character of a man is reflected in his ability to love and care for a child. If he can do that, he is truly unselfish. He's the kind of man who genuinely finds joy by putting the needs of another ahead of his own. This is real strength of character, not the man in constant pursuit of money, fame and power to validate his existence and worth. In my opinion, such goals are a sad indication of low self-esteem and great lack of maturity. John is one of the good guys, someone I can count on and it didn't take me long to realize I had a "keeper," as my father used to say. We've been together ever since that Thursday in January and have been married for over 20 years.

He's the love of my life and my BFF. He repeated his question again, only more forcefully, "Are you **absolutely** sure you're alright?"

I couldn't keep my concerns secret any longer and spilled the beans, but only told him about repeating some blood work. Why get all upset when bad news remained a **possibility**, not a **reality**.

By Monday afternoon, new blood results still hadn't been posted on the Kaiser site and neither had the findings from the chest X-ray, yet I didn't take this as anything too out of the ordinary. I figured the weekend had slowed things down in the busy medical profession. When the phone rang I jumped though, hoping, really hoping, there was good news on the other end. Again it was from my doctor's office.

The nurse said a time had been arranged the next day for me and a family member to come to Kaiser and speak with my internist. The second blood tests had validated the first. I suddenly felt a giant gut check. Things I'd researched on the internet rang like a bell in my head, and the only word out of my mouth was a wimpy, "Okay." Then I quickly asked, "Any news about the X-ray?"

"That's something you can discuss with the doctor too," she stated.

I leveled with John about everything; making public the phone calls and their contents, the tests and especially my fears, now heightened even more because the nurse told me to bring a family member to my upcoming appointment. We cuddled on the couch and held each other tight, the way people do when a terrible disaster is about to strike.

John and I were sitting in my doctor's examination room at 11:00 am the next morning. We waited about 15 minutes before Dr. Grau hurried into his domain of brown walls and florescent lighting. His posture was erect, his demeanor, detached. He made uncomfortable eye contact with John first and then me. He'd been my physician for a couple years, but I hardly knew him.

"How are you today?" his question hollow inside the four walls.

"Not real good," I answered. "What's wrong with me?" I figured cutting to the chase was my best strategy to find out what I needed to know and the fastest way to make an informed exit home. He re-adjusted his tie and pushed his thick glasses up higher against the small bridge of his nose, clearing the way for me to get a better look at his baby blues. Then he spoke quickly and in a matter-of-fact tone, like he was ordering his usual latte at Starbucks and was late for an appointment.

"I'm sorry to have to tell you this, but it appears you have leukemia, Chronic Lymphocytic Leukemia. Abnormal lymphocytes, unlike the normal ones in your blood, aren't dying off like they should. Instead, they are accumulating in your blood stream and unfortunately taking up space needed for the healthy ones. Eventually, though usually at a slow rate, you may start to develop secondary symptoms that your body finds difficult to handle. For right now it appears your only symptom of CLL is the large number of lymphocytes appearing in your blood, so I recommend what is called 'watchful waiting.' We'll keep a close eye on your condition and have you repeat blood tests about every 3 months or so to monitor the leukemia's progression." He paused from his rapid-fire explanation and waited for my response, his glasses renewing their downward slip.

Even though its probability had come up during my research yesterday, the word "leukemia" hit me hard and with a paralyzing affect. John gripped my hand as we sat side by side in Grau's windowless exam room. I longed more than ever to glimpse the outside world as my inside world collapsed around me, but I couldn't. The good doctor offered a Kleenex from the miniature box on the counter, expecting the single drop that had met my cheek signaled a river to come. But it didn't come. I shut down and plunged into stoic mode.

"I read that high WBC and lymphocyte numbers sometimes also indicate hepatitis or mono. Could it be one of those instead of leukemia?" I asked, hoping for the less dire diagnosis.

He returned the Kleenex to the counter and said matter-of-factly, "No. In the last blood draw we tested for those two things. It's leukemia,

Chronic Lymphocytic Leukemia. I've had my colleagues also examine your blood work. But know this," he stated with conviction. "If you have to have leukemia, CLL is the best kind compared to the others. Many patients don't even need treatment for the disease in their lifetimes because it can progress so slowly. And your chest X-ray is normal; that's excellent. No infections or tumors in the lungs, so let's all hope for the best." He took another breath and searched my eyes for a hint of relief. "We need to do some additional tests to find out more about your specific type of CLL though and I want to refer you to an oncologist in town. Do you have a preference?"

"No. Is there someone you recommend?" I asked, my spirits lifting ever so slightly.

"Salem Oncology and Hemotology have some fine physicians. I'll refer you to someone there." He quickly scribbled a notation on my chart and checked his watch.

The whole conversation was surreal, like all three of us were talking about some stranger, not me. Even after two rounds of blood tests, a chest X-ray, hours of research on the internet, a diagnosis from Dr. Grau and his colleagues and my need to see a cancer specialist, I struggled with the reality of the situation.

Then John questioned the doctor, "What kind of tests?"

Grau set my chart down and answered with, "I want to order a test that determines the cell surface markers by flow cytometry on a new peripheral blood sample and send it to Oregon Health Sciences University in Portland. That test will tell us important information about your specific type of CLL. Each person's leukemia is unique and each person will react to his or her leukemia in unique ways." Grau took a breath and then asked politely, "How do you feel about another blood draw, right now?"

I looked at John and he looked at me and together we nodded, "Yes."

"Good. Also, have you experienced any unusual fatigue, night sweats, fevers or swollen lymph nodes you're aware of?" Grau's pen was ready for action again.

"No." I came back. "Should I?"

"Not necessarily, especially this early in the game. Now, I'd like to examine you, alright?" After I gave my consent, he squirted soap in both hands and gave each a vigorous washing.

With his clean fingers he then gently applied pressure to the sides of my neck, above my clavicle, in my armpits, and over my liver and spleen. "Your spleen feels a little enlarged. Any pain in that area?" he asked with friendly concern.

"No, not really," I said, making a mental note to keep track of swelling or pain in any of the body parts he'd touched.

"Good. Good," he stated quickly. "Sometimes an enlarged spleen occurs in CLL patients because the spleen is really one big lymph node." He eyed my husband, wanting to keep him in the conversation. "Now, before you head to the lab, I made copies from an internet site Kaiser makes available for patients with your diagnosis, and it'd be helpful if you'd both read it carefully. To start coming to a better understanding of the disease," he added.

He handed the 15 page document to me and I glanced at its title, 'Initial Treatment of Chronic Lymphocytic Leukemia.' Suddenly everything was all too real.

"And you'll be hearing from me within the next few days about that referral to a hematologist/oncologist. Head over to the lab and they'll take care of you."

Kaiser Permanente's recommended 12 minutes with Dr. Grau had concluded. He turned and walked briskly out of the room, hurrying over to a closed door across the hall, knocking before gaining swift admittance to see his next patient. John and I were alone in the hallway, and for the first time since we'd arrived, I noticed the pungent medical smell of the world around me, not at all like home.

John pointed me toward the lab for another draw, with another rubber band, another red ball and another butterfly needle. I'd be getting to know the threesome better, and better; that was a given. As the purple liquid flowed once more from my vein through the needle into the large tube and travelled into the narrow vials, I sadly realized the good doc had NOT once called me Pam, not even Mrs. Johnson.

Back home I rearranged the pillows on my bed and got comfy as I started reading about the new me, courtesy of Kaiser's handout. I was no longer the woman who just had breast cancer, now I was also the woman who had leukemia too. True, we're not simply the sum of our bodies' diseases, but to a large extent our health challenges dictate how we live our lives. Doctor visits become commonplace, tests and procedures become routine, and setbacks shadow our days. I dove head first into page 1 and right off the bat didn't like what I learned.

CLL was presently incurable and if I started treatment early, before any secondary symptoms became problematic, my long-term survival wouldn't improve. So no wonder I was in the watch and wait phase.

As I read further, I learned about the staging in leukemia. Because I didn't yet exhibit weakness, night sweats, weight loss, painful lymph nodes or fever, was not anemic, hadn't experienced episodes of infection requiring antibiotics, or appeared to have a dangerously high lymphocyte count which was doubling, I was in stage 1 of 4.

When to begin treatment was uncertain in many cases depending on the severity of secondary symptoms and the overall health of patients like myself. Before a decision was made, I'd have to undergo further blood tests and probably a bone marrow biopsy to determine treatment options. I didn't like the sound of "bone biopsy" at all. Just the probability of having one made shivers run down my spine.

The document then started listing possible treatment scenarios, like combining chemo drugs Fludarabine plus Rituximab (FR), which resulted in unpleasant side-effects of fever, chills, nausea, vomiting, etc. The list of drugs went on and on with longer and longer names, and their toxic levels described in more detail than my emotional state of mind could handle. I took a break from all the leukemia stuff and showered so I could get rid of the odor of Grau's office and Kaiser in general. Then I resumed my reading.

Experts agreed my diseased lymphocytes could be killed off with treatment, but not all would face the death penalty. Those that remained would multiply and stay alive, enlarging my lymph nodes, hurting my ability to fight all kinds of infections, damaging my organs and ultimately causing secondary symptoms to do what leukemia does so well, kill people. A tiny paragraph mixed in with this news was brief mention about clinical trials offering hope to people with CLL.

The last few pages, along with an article I'd downloaded by Chaya Venkat and titled, 'Infections in CLL: Who is Most at Risk,' especially interested me because they talked about precautions I could employ to improve my odds of not getting infections, the most deadly of secondary symptoms. Some pieces of advice were to get medical attention right away if I felt ill, because I needed to stay out of hospitals where nasty resistant super bugs abounded, just waiting to attack my weakened immune system. And to help make sure of this, it was crucial to have broad spectrum antibiotics like Amoxicillin and Azithromycin on hand.

Good hygiene was also very important, both for me and family members with whom I came in contact. Frequent and thorough hand washings with warm water and soap or use of hand sanitizers whose active ingredient was 70% ethyl alcohol was paramount. Products such as Clorox and Lysol wipes were advised for phones, door handles, computer keyboards, iPads, counters, etc. Clearly, I was doing myself a favor by becoming a world class cleaning machine.

Hard to accept but necessary, was the info about grandchildren. The articles said they were 'germ magnets' who must be avoided when they had even the slightest of sniffles, and more so when they had any kind of fever. My compromised system meant less time with Sydney and Aiden; in fact, if I wanted to stay well I really shouldn't be around ANYONE who didn't have an absolute clean bill of health. B..U..M..M..E..R!

After reading those recommendations, the next day I bought LOTS and LOTS of bottles of Purell, "the #1 brand in hospitals that kills more than 99.9 % of germs." I started carrying one in my purse, a couple in our car, placed them in strategic places around the house, and even tucked a miniature in my tennis bag. Dirty tennis balls and hands soaked in sweat after matches were no longer innocent of consequences for me; they could lead to bad infections from which I might not recover.

Other pieces of advice were to get a flu shot early in the season, as well as pneumonia shots recommended by my doctors. No shingles shots though because they contained a live virus which could make me sicker than a dog.

The list of do's and don'ts continued, and I read and re-read them. Things like leaving Charlie's litter box for my husband to clean was now a must, as well as putting my pet in the garage at night instead of keeping his furry body next to me in bed. Garden gloves were required when I did yard work and if I ever got even the littlest of cuts or insects bites, I was instructed to clean the wound well and immediately apply antibiotic ointment.

Some of the most important things I needed to do were saved for last in the handout. They were to call a doctor immediately if my temperature ever got to "the danger zone" of 100.4 and wouldn't go down with Tylenol or extra hydration, take four, 500 mg tablets of Amoxicillin one hour before any dental work to prevent infection, and ALWAYS wear sun block with an ultra violet sun protection rating of at least 30 because CLL patients were especially susceptible to a wide range of skin cancers.

All of these precautions, although they were many, were common sense, smart, and well worth the effort they entailed. Like everyone else I wanted to stay well as long as I could, not just for myself, but my entire family. I didn't want my husband to be without a wife; I didn't want my daughter to be without a mother; I didn't want my grandchildren to be without their grandmother. I'd learned a long time ago, 1997 to be exact, that cancer is a family disease even when only a single member has it.

Not mentioned in the Kaiser handout, but a well known way to stop the spread of any contagion, is the distancing of one's self from other people. With that in mind, the long held practice of John and I sleeping in different bedrooms had been a wise one, even though our decision to do so was for vastly different reasons.

To bring on a restful sleep John loves listening to audio books such as John LeCarre's TINKER, TAILOR, SOLDIER, SPY and George R. R.

Martin's SONG of FIRE and ICE, as well watching old, classic science fiction movies. One of his favorite and often watched films from childhood is THE SHE CREATURE, and because of his constant tinnitus, my husband loves SHE and all volumes of everything well above my comfort zone.

I, on the other hand, must have quiet to fall asleep; the absence of noise, words, loud male snoring, and things that go bump in the night. My sleep inducers, free of annoying ear-plugs and the medium of TV, DVD's and CD players, are non-fiction books, historical novels, and solitaire on my tablet. We love one another dearly, but sleep deprivation can drive a person bonkers, and going without sleep puts the kibosh on love-making faster than separate bedrooms ever did.

By separating at nighttime we don't get one another sick like we always used to. No longer is it a given that John comes down with a cold and I'm sure to follow, or I get a sore throat and Johnny wakes up with the same. It's wonderful for a husband and wife to share things in a marriage, but contagions definitely aren't one of them.

A few days after ingesting all the handout had to offer and failed attempts at putting leukemia aside, giving me some light in this darkness was the results of a special CLL FISH panel Grau had ordered before I moved from him to Strother at Salem Hematology. FISH stands for "fluorescence in situ hybridization" and it looks for gene changes in cells. Genes are made of DNA which controls everything the cell does, including when it grows and reproduces. This special blood test showed I had DNA that reflected deletion 13q-Abnormal. In layman's terms, it meant that when treatment was required, it most likely would be effective. That was good news to these old ears. I thrived on finding something to be hopeful about; all cancer patients do.

I received a referral to Dr. John Strother a short time later and soon he became my friend and "watchful waiting" partner. He monitored my blood work and growing spleen very carefully every 3 months, and we'd have long talks about CLL; he always remembered my name too.

From July of 2009-2010, my test results stayed pretty stable, with WBC count and # of lymphocytes increasing ever so slightly. But people like me with CLL can suddenly, and without reason, experience big increases in their numbers. It's almost like we're little kids who go through a growth spurt and that's exactly what happened in 2011.

I remembered from all my extensive study of CLL and corroborated by Dr. Strother, that a doubling of lymphocyte numbers within a 6 month period spelled real trouble. Thank God my increase wasn't quite that bad, but I could feel my spleen getting bigger and bigger. It felt like a balloon had inflated inside my body and was pressing against my rib cage. I even had to discard my belted jeans for size 16 Lane Bryant slacks with an adjustable drawstring.

In early 2013, my WBC count was 72.7 with a double "HH" in the flag column and my lymphocyte number was 98 with a single "H." Nearby, a comment read: "Majority of lymphs appear normal." That meant most of my lymphocytes remained healthy, but a whole lot of unhealthy and abnormal ones also flowed through my bloodstream and many decided to home themselves in my spleen. I felt like I was pregnant, only the baby wasn't moving and it wasn't in my uterus. I even named her, "Pammie," a bit of sick humor no one but me found funny. Dr. Strother's probing of my little girl during examinations became more and more uncomfortable, so we finally decided to size her up by way of some CT scans.

On February 13, 2013, one such scan at Salem Hospital stated, "borderline mild splenomegaly." If what I was feeling was only mild, I sure as heck wasn't looking forward to the next medical stage of moderate or worse yet, severe. My poor spleen, normally fist size, was going on double and I started having trouble on the tennis court with my overhead smash. Every time I reached my racket up high with my right arm, I'd pay with follow-through pain on my left side. Pammie was unforgiving in her message of, "Don't do that anymore!" And my once strong overhead serve was a thing of the past. It hurt my spleen too much, so I perfected an underhand spin serve that drove my mixed opponents crazy, especially the male of the species. Men love to show their prowess by blasting female serves back over the net, but mine curved away from them and often looped entirely off the court with them sprinting to get to it. They glared back at me like, "What the hell kind of serve is that!" I smiled back at my partner, and Johnny always smiled back at me.

Tennis was my sport; it brought a real normalcy to the abnormalities of life with leukemia, and I desperately wanted to continue doing what I loved, hitting that little yellow ball across the net. But my playing days didn't last long, even with avoiding overheads and serving underhand. Those darn lymphocytes were collecting in my blood stream faster and faster, and Dr. Strother said a fall on the courts or an opponent hitting a hard ball at my "baby" might cause rupture and then I could lose my body's strongest infection fighting organ. If I wasn't scared enough already by my CLL, I sure was now. I said a fond farewell to tennis and wondered if I'd every return to the one sport I was really good at, the one sport my husband and I had played together for 35 years.

Two thousand thirteen was a real turning point in my care for more reasons than just the progression of my CLL. First, Kaiser Permanente changed their health coverage and stopped approving outside referrals for patients. I couldn't continue seeing Dr. Strother and I was heartbroken. He was the one who helped me stay hopeful by reassuring me over and over again that I'd be around to see my grandkids graduate from high school and that I'd have years to grow old with my young husband. Even though each visit with him spoke of higher and higher numbers and a bigger and bigger spleen, defeat was not my game plan. He made sure of that.

Having left Strother, I saw a Kaiser oncologist for a little while by the name of Dr. Rarick, a highly competent and pleasant man as I recall. But when I turned 65 years old and selected MODA Medicare Advantage, I found better care at lower prices and the best part of the deal, I could select my own doctors. My first priority, finding a doctor whose PRECISE specialty was Chronic Lymphocytic Leukemia.

Dr. Strother had taken good care of me and I thank him to this day. But my leukemia's advancement would soon out-pace its "watch and wait" period, and I wanted to be the patient of an expert so good in the treatment of CLL that doctors everywhere consulted him for his advice and treatment of my kind of blood cancer. Luckily I found Dr. Jeffrey Porter Sharman. And I found him on the internet, of course!

Dr. Sharman practices at the Willamette Valley Cancer Institute and Research Center in the Eugene/Springfield area 65 miles south of Keizer, and is medical director of hematology research for the US Oncology Network. One of his specialties is Chronic Lymphocytic Leukemia and when I called his office I was politely told he was taking new patients. Maybe, just maybe, I could be one of those lucky individuals.

Dr. Sharman's medical background is impressive, to say the least. He went to medical school at the University of California, Davis, with Internship and Residency at Harvard's Massachusetts General. He also completed a Fellowship at Stanford University and presently was involved in different leukemia clinical trials, all of which showed great promise. Checking him out further, I watched videos from his internet site, and needless to say I liked what I saw...a VERY smart man who was not only brilliant but personable, a guy I could put my trust in like Strother and who knew my disease, really knew MY disease. I felt like a miner who'd just struck gold. Or better yet, a patient who had just found her way to a longer survival rate.

I called the Willamette Valley Cancer Institute and Research Center again and booked my first appointment. I was informed of a $20.00 co-pay and that I was also required to FAX all my medical records having to do with CLL to Sharman's office ASAP. The staff person told me that the doctor always insisted on reviewing patient cases prior to his initial meeting with them. Following instructions like a good student in my own classroom, I did as I was told, gathering up everything relevant to my leukemia and making copies at Kinko's to the tune of $65.00. I waited patiently at a FAX machine until I received a message that all pages had gone though and then drove home to celebrate with a glass of wine and barefoot stroll across the beach in our backyard. Yes, a real beach with coastal sand, palm trees and seashells in the middle of none other than Keizer, OR, miles from the Pacific Ocean. "Life was good." I was enjoying the beach, Sharman was my doctor, and turning old finally had the advantage of Medicare coverage. What could go wrong?

When the date for my appointment arrived, my husband insisted on driving me. He'd grown up in Springfield, and was familiar with the area and also Eugene, located right next door. More important than knowing the way, he wanted to be by my side when this new doctor took over my care. Always protective and loving, John, to this day, is the best thing that's ever happened to me.

We parked the car and rode the elevator to the 5th floor and Sharman's office. Sitting in reception at the WVCI, we were surrounded by patients with bald heads and far- away looks in their eyes. One whole wall of reception was windows and they let in the beautiful sunshine of early spring in Oregon. In a fenced field on the other side of the clinic's parking lot was a skinny, light beige colored horse all alone nibbling on a bale of hay, a little touch of country in my city of cancer. On a round table filtered by the glorious light was a 1000 piece puzzle of a beautiful pond full of water lilies; all but a few stray pieces missing from the scene. Magazines were stacked on tables next to newly upholstered chairs, and coffee and tea stood ready for anyone so inclined. The whole area was quiet and comforting, except for the sad-eyed patients who looked me over, knowing I was the new person on the block who'd just moved into their gated community of chemo treatments.

Before long my name was called for blood work and I settled into a chair in the lab, just down the hall from the coffee machine. "Here we go again," I thought. The person placed a latex glove full of hot water on my left arm and tied a stretchy around my upper arm. She quickly readied the butterfly needle without any request on my part, and asked me for my name and date of birth.

"Pam Johnson, 2-28-48," I said. With just one poke, she found a good vein and I was out of there in nothing flat, walking back to John who was still reading the same article in SPORTS ILLUSTRATED as when I left. Patients nearby had broken their silence and were conversing like old friends and enjoying the hot beverages. Two gentlemen had teamed up and were close to finishing the puzzle, and one lady was busy knitting a pretty hat. John looked up from his magazine and shot me a grin. Right away I knew this place was going to be okay.

After watching the horse another few minutes, I was in Dr. Sharman's office with a nurse taking my blood pressure, temperature, and pulse. She went to her computer and asked me about my present medications; got them all recorded, and stated that my medical records had been downloaded and were safely in my chart files. Talk about efficiency. She said Sharman would be in soon, smiled at me, and closed the door softly. John and I let out a simultaneous sigh of relief.

A moment later in walked Dr. Sharman, a handsome man in his early 40's, who appeared happy with himself and glad to be at work that day. He shook both our hands with a firm grip and asked, "How can I help you Pam?" He would have had me at "Hello" if this was the movie, JERRY McGUIRE and I was Rene Zellwigger. Yep. I'd found my guy alright.

Our visit lasted 45 minutes and he never once looked at his watch. He knew all about me from my records and better yet, the blood work I'd just done at his lab was already in his computer and a copy was being run off as we spoke. He reached the conclusion that I should remain in the "watch and wait" stage, and encouraged me to go about my life, stay active even without playing tennis, and at all costs, avoid sick people. My hubby and I had all our questions answered and avoided posing hypothetical ones. We said our good-byes. Little did I know something bad was on the horizon. Yes, a whole lot of shit was ready to hit the fan!

A few months before meeting Sharman and while still with Dr. Strother, I noticed a cyst-like growth on the left side of my cheek, on the face, (not my behind). Since I was prone to developing cysts elsewhere on my body, I didn't think too much about another one popping up and figured I'd have it removed at my leisure, I'd done so with all the others.

I had a dermatologist take a look at it when the bump quickly started getting bigger, and she recommended a series of steroid injections to decrease the inflammation prior to surgically removing it in her office. After one injection and the lesion not getting any smaller and me noticing two others above and below the primary one, I knew something wasn't right. Call it woman's intuition, or whatever, but this was no ordinary cyst.

To make a long story short, I had surgery at Oregon Health and Science University in August of 2013, for removal of multiple facial tumors, all found to be Merkel cell carcinoma, one of the rarest and most aggressive types of skin cancer known to mankind. Yes, the shit had really hit the fan and hit it hard!

My surgeon in Portland was Dr. Peter Andersen, a highly skilled physician in the Otolaryngology Department. He removed not only the primary tumor, two satellite ones, and left salivary gland, but 44 nearby lymph nodes in my neck to check for Merkel metastasis. Fortunately, pathology tests showed the cancer hadn't spread beyond my cheek.

Andersen is a great guy, one of those even-keeled people whose hands are so steady he would have made a great gunslinger in the old West. When I first saw Dr. A, I swore he was the spitting image of the older brother on the TV series, FRAISER, played by Kelsey Grammar. Mentioning the close similarity, the doctor didn't appear too surprised, but then I don't think much ever surprises Andersen. The scar left from my Merkel surgery, all 86 stitches of it, now blends well into my deep smile lines and the wrinkles of my neck. I decided against plastic surgery and a 5 day stay in a germy hospital.

Between surgery at OHSU and 30 Merkel radiation treatments at Salem Hospital under the supervision of Dr. Kang, John and I had a consultation with Dr. Paul Nghiem at the Seattle Cancer Care Alliance in Washington. He's one of only a handful of doctors in the entire world who is considered an expert in Merkel diagnosis and treatment, so it's no wonder I'd been misdiagnosed earlier by my dermatologist. Nghiem was especially helpful in planning my radiation regiment, as well as allowing me into his study of Merkel antibodies as a way to monitor recurrence or spread of the disease. A few times a year I agreed to have vials of my blood drawn and sent to his University of Washington lab for analysis of the antibodies whose numbers indicated any cancer activity within my body. I was more than glad to do this...it helped him in his study, and it acted as an early warning system for me.

I continued seeing Dr. Sharman, my ace in the hole, and with MODA my insurance of choice, was able to also see Dr. Strother for occasional blood draws and consultations in Salem. But as fate would have it, my numbers were in the hundreds by late 2014, my red blood cells were being affected, my platelets were going down, I was bruising more easily, and I was starting to feel a little "off." Not quite like myself. "Billy Jean Spleen," as she'd been renamed in honor of the great tennis pro, also felt like she was close to full term and ready to burst. A decision had to be made, but not without the dreaded Merkel taken into consideration also.

All the statistical data on my kind of skin cancer said the likelihood of it returning dropped tremendously if none had reappeared after 2 years from diagnosis. In 2014, I wasn't yet at 2 years. I contacted Dr. Nghiem in Seattle and explained that my CLL doctors were talking about treatment options and I asked for his opinion. He was adamant about his patients not having chemotherapy treatments for other diseases unless their oncologists said it was absolutely necessary because MAYBE such treatments could bring about a Merkel recurrence. So that was my dilemma. Start chemo before I hit the magic number of being 2 years free of Merkel, or wait until at least July of 2015 and hope I'd still be strong enough to handle the leukemia treatments ahead of me.

I still felt pretty good...no infections, no night sweats, no temperatures and no serious fatigue, but would I stay that way. That was the million dollar question, and without a crystal ball no one knew the answer. Life, for all of us, is full of tough decisions and one was staring me right smack in the face.

During a very serious visit with Dr. Sharman in early 2015, we talked about Merkel being the disease most likely to cut my life short in the quickest possible way. To quote him exactly, "Merkel is the real elephant in the room, Pam." He reminded me again that people with CLL had a way of sticking around the longest of all leukemia patients, but I also knew that putting off treatment too long could hurt my chances of it being successful. He was worried about that too.

Ultimately, when to start treatment was going to be left up to me. So after many a sleepless night and long talks with John, I decided to do something I'd never been good at, waiting.

PRE-TRIAL ASSESSMENTS

In April I had a heart to heart with Dr. Strother and new blood work done at his office. My WBC now registered "critical high" with a number of 149.41, my lymphocyte count was 143.50, my red blood cell numbers dropped lower and platelets followed suit. A recent scan showed my spleen bulging at more than 2 times its normal size, with a radiologist stating in the report that my splenomegaly had moved from moderate to "prominent." So goes the life of a CLL patient who'd been watching and waiting for almost 6 years. Even though I'd been expecting the news, seeing it written so coldly in black and white got to me.

"Well Pam, it's time," said Strother.

"You're right," I mourned. Dr Sharman had said the same thing only 2 weeks earlier. Both men were on the same page and that put me there too.

"I know Dr. Sharman is your CLL specialist, but OHSU is enrolling people in a clinical trial whose Chronic Lymphocytic Leukemia has not yet been treated. Going through a trial might get you better results than conventional methods of treatment, although with any trial not all of the side-effects are known and there are certainly dangers involved. Would you be willing to see an oncologist there?"

My answer stalled. All I could think about was him using the words, "side-effects" and "dangers," and wishing I could go home.

"Pam, what do you think?" repeated Strother, calling me back for an answer.

"As much as I don't want to start treatment, I know it's time. Guess I'm greedy. I wanted more than 6 years."

"It'll be okay," he reassured me. "This clinical trial could very well offer you an amazing opportunity to be on the cutting edge of controlling CLL and eventually curing it. I can't make any guarantees, but if it were me, I'd sure do it."

"What if it was someone you loved?"

"Without a second thought," he said firmly. "Without a second thought."

So the following week John and I were on our way to see Dr. Alexey Danilov at Oregon Health and Science University in Portland. He was the oncologist/hematologist from Russia who would soon be heading a Phase II clinical trial for people like me. He'd attended Jaroslavl State Medical Academy in the motherland of Putin and more recently the Geisel School of Medicine at Dartmouth.

Yes, I checked him out before our visit; I strongly believe that everyone should check out their doctors, always and carefully. It's called being smart about who we employ to perform the service of keeping us alive to enjoy our days six feet above, instead of six feet under. We certainly check Angie's List for the best plumber in our area, we read CONSUMER'S DIGEST to find out which Ford has a five star safety rating, and we don't hesitate clicking on Home Advisor before calling a tree service. Due diligence is never a bad idea and I'm forever appalled at the number of people who do none of it.

During the appointment we had a good talk and I liked his relaxed demeanor and Russian accent. He reviewed my case out loud to us, and I had no doubt he was up on my most recent test results. He gave me a thorough exam, verifying my swollen spleen and enlarged lymph nodes along the sides of my neck and above my clavicle.

He told me the trial would be combining, for the FIRST time, two drugs previously used only separately. They were Bendamustine and Obinutuzumab, commonly referred to as Gazyva. The Phase I study had included about 50 patients across the United States, and now a Phase II study had been approved to include more than that. I remembered thinking to myself that I'd be keeping company with a very select group of men and women; we'd be trying something never attempted before, and it'd be dangerous.

The voice of Captain Kirk echoed silently about the room, with me hearing each word clearly. "Space: the final frontier. These are the voyages of the starship Enterprise. Its five year mission: to explore strange new worlds, to seek out new life and new civilizations, to boldly go where no man has gone before." The hairs on my arms stood at attention, just like his Mr. Spock.

It wasn't difficult figuring out Danilov was knowledgeable about CLL. He knew Dr. Sharman personally and respected the research he'd been doing about my disease and the many clinical trials already taking place in Springfield and Eugene. Danilov confirmed that my FISH test indicated treatment would be effective and that the time to begin was now. Watch and wait was without question, over. He asked if he could do a blood test that would include a "Gene Trails Hematologic Malignancies 76 Gene Panel." This was a highly sophisticated means to help determine further if the Phase II study combining Bendamustine and Gazyva would likely assure success in my specific type of CLL. The consent form paragraph explained:

> This test is designed to detect alterations in the 76 genes, many of whom are known to play a role in leukemia/lymphoma pathogenesis, prognosis or response to therapy. Genomic DNA is extracted and purified from blood or bone marrow.

On the drive back home to Keizer, I nursed a very sore left arm. The young phlebotomist poked me five times before finding the right vein to draw enough blood for not only the gene trails test, but also a complete metabolic panel and CBC with white cell differential, automated. At least the poker was a hunk and smelled of Old Spice, but his repeated pokes drove me crazy and Danilov wasn't happy either, shooting Mr. Spice an evil eye on his 4th attempt. Bruises decorated my poor arm for a whole week, lasting longer than the temporary tattoos and henna

Syd and I decorated ourselves with the month before.

The next day I told John I wanted to see Dr. Sharman and find out what he had to say about this clinical trial. Not that I didn't connect with, or that I harbored ill feelings about the poor blood sucker employed at OHSU, but something just told me to get to Springfield before I committed to Portland. This was too important a decision not to be explored a little more.

The Sharman appointment was set, but before going to it Danilov's office called. They told me my gene trails test showed I was a prime candidate for their clinical trial, but and this was a BIG but, OHSU wouldn't be starting their trial for a while. When I pressed the caller for how long a "while" was, the lady couldn't give me a straight answer. The idea of visiting Sharman was definitely the smart thing to do.

Returning to his office this time around I felt even more comfortable. I was used to the surroundings and this took away some of my apprehension traveling a trial. I liked that the two receptionists were the friendly faces who'd greeted me before and the soft music playing was the same old elevator tunes. The nearby rest room toilets flushed with their usual great water pressure; Earl Gray and Jasmine Mint were again the tea offerings, and a puzzle once more spread itself on the same round table by the window. The entire place had a wonderful familiarity; the kind I could depend on to help alleviate my fears and anxiety, and if called upon, maybe even a panic attack or two. Most importantly, my horse was still in the pasture.

My wounded left arm was poked, but again success was achieved on the first try with help from a blessed butterfly and warm water inside a surgical glove. Once in with Sharman, my hubby and I told him all about our visit at OHSU and Dr. Danilov, whom he remembered talking with months earlier. I also handed him a copy of the CBC blood work and told him about the gene trail testing. I hit pay dirt when Sharman told me they had already started the exact same clinical trial right there at WVCI and he wanted me to seriously consider joining his, rather than Danilov's.

If I chose his, I'd have the answer to "when" and be under the care of a great doctor who I knew well. Also, we'd be avoiding the crowded freeway traffic to and from Portland; instead, we'd be traveling a road less traveled by, going to a city my husband knew like the back of his hand. The decision seemed like a no brainer.

Sharman entered my quiet thoughts with, "You and I already agree that treatment needs to start soon and, according to my records, you're just about two years out from your Merkel diagnosis with no recurrence. That's encouraging, so what do you think, Pam?"

Feeling slightly disloyal to Danilov but realizing all the advantages of a clinical trial at WVCI, I replied, "Yes, let's do it!"

Immediately, Sharman left the room, and in under a minute returned with a lovely dark-haired young woman who held a stack of medical folders close to her chest. "I'd like you to meet Betty, our clinical trial nurse who coordinates things for our patients and is with them every step of the way as they ready for a trial."

"Hi Pam, I'm Betty and understand you're considering our CLL trial. Would you like to see our treatment room?"

Wow! Things were going fast. Not moving an inch in the direction of THE ROOM, I hesitated; feeling like what I really wanted to do was duck in the corner and draw up into a fetal position. Or maybe run to the garage like Charlie always did when he spied the kitty carrier to take him to Keizer Veterinary Clinic for another visit with Dr. Hatch. My instincts said, "flee", but my reasoning powers said, "be brave and get with the program." I looked at Betty and asked, "Can my husband come too?"

"Sure, no problem; come this way," she said slowly, her words more in tune with my pace of acceptance. We followed her across reception and through a door into the treatment area. My first reaction as I scanned the place was, "Oh, God. I don't know if I can do this." The room was packed with patients all sitting in brown recliners, their arms and chests hooked up to tubes that slowly dripped, dripped, dripped different colored drugs. This was going to be hard, really, really hard, and I was taken aback by the challenge ahead. My face grew pale and my palms turned ice cold. It was like I was a 12 year old all over again, sitting in Salem's old Elsinore Theatre watching HORROR OF DRACULA and waiting for the prince of darkness to sink his fangs into my jugular.

"I know it's a lot at first," Betty said as she looked at me, a reassuring smile working its way across her kind face. "You'll get used to it; I promise you will. And we're all here to help."

She walked us slowly around the large room, and I listened to the many nurses and patients chatting about anti-nausea meds, the best cold spray for use before inserting needles in ports, blood counts going up and down, number of bags finished in how many minutes, and the cleverest way to navigate a bathroom break while still hooked up to chemo bags. No one was crying or grimacing in pain. No one was vomiting on the floor or fainting in their chairs. Things seemed so normal, in what to me was a totally abnormal environment that I relaxed, kind of.

We strolled by a small kitchen area housing a Kenmore frig stocked with juices and water, and a counter crowded with Wheat Thins and a box of Saltines. These things, along with that day's homemade goods of chocolate chip cookies, cinnamon rolls and doughnuts, and a cake with "Thank You" printed across the frosting, sat ready for everybody to enjoy. As part of the treatment area there were also two large private rooms and two bathrooms big enough to accommodate wheel chairs. The nurse's station was a round configuration, crowded with computers and people checking orders and patient files. Behind the station was a pharmacy where drugs were mixed and verified by technicians and made ready for treatment nurses to administer.

"What's that sign doing on the back of that recliner?" I was pointing to 'RESERVED' on the chair closest to the nurses' station and parked right in the middle of the biggest window with the best view of the old horse eating clover.

"That's for a first timer; someone who is starting chemo this afternoon."

"Hum, the best seat in the house," I thought, and then quickly felt terrified at the realization I would soon be its next occupant.

We slowly continued our walk around the big room and I stared at the patients undergoing their treatments. Many sat beneath blankets drawn up tight to their chins, napping; others visited with one another or with loved ones sitting in chairs pulled close by. Some were reading, quietly talking on their cell phones or glued to their iPads. A few were knitting and drawing.

My attention was drawn to one young woman who was stuffing wedding invitations into envelopes and reminding her mother to call the florist at the Gateway Mall about the cost of tulips and baby's breath. She was very happy and kept holding up her hand, admiring the diamond engagement ring on her left finger. I especially liked the colorful turban covering her head; its African design was stunning and allowed small black curls to sneak out onto the side of her face and back of her neck. Mother and daughter were in their wonderful world of wedding preparations, very distant from the battlefield of cancer.

"She's getting married in a few months," said Betty looking at me looking at them. "It's good to bring things to help you keep your mind off of treatment and make the time go faster." Then she added, "Patients often complain about boredom."

"I'll take boring any day," I returned.

"We could play cribbage, or cards," said my husband, a hint of enthusiasm in his voice. We liked playing five-handed Pinochle and for now my grandma record of wins overshadowed his grandpa losses. Perhaps he was planning a comeback.

"So, what do you think?" asked Betty.

Looking at John who was in full agreement, I said, "I think I'd like to do the clinical trial here and not OHSU." Any loyalty to Danilov had quickly disappeared in favor of my hubby's hometown and knickname of its athletic teams, the Springfield Millers. Also, my great comfort with Sharman, Betty, and the Willamette Cancer Institute and Research Center was becoming more and more my "safe place;" like a panic room in the midst of an attack.

"Good. Sharman is a wonderful doctor, and every one of the nurses has been doing this for years and will take excellent care of you." She guided us to her office.

John and I scooted our chairs together across from Betty and leaned forward to listen carefully. She said the trial title was "Phase II, Open-Label Study of Obinutuzumab Plus Bendamustine (BG) in Patients with Previously Untreated Chronic Lymphocytic Leukemia." This meant that I'd be one of a few hundred patients in the trial nationwide who hadn't yet been treated for CLL, and all of us and our health care providers would be aware of the specific drugs administered. Placebos, substances having no pharmacological effect, would NOT be used. Two drugs, Obinutuzumab (a monoclonal antibody) and Bendamustine (an alkylating agent which interfers with the DNA in cancer cells) would be **combined** for the first time to determine their therapeutic success for patients like myself. A Phase I trial had already been completed with fewer patients enrolled and its results showed promise, along with manageable side-effects.

Now a Phase II was in place, and I wanted to be part of it, but I wasn't going to be accepted into the clinical trial simply because I passed the FISH test with flying colors, or liked the idea of the biotechnology company Genentech footing the bill for $60,000 worth of drugs and a lot of my treatment costs. No, I had to go through thorough screening to determine if I met the criteria for inclusion in the six month study.

That meant I MUST agree to things like extensive and routine testing of my blood, repeated bone marrow aspirations rather than biopsies, CT's and MRI's, electrocardiograms, complete physical exams, and detailed medical updates regarding my changing health status. In addition, I was required to have follow- up visits with Sharman and his research team every three months for three years after the completion of my chemotherapy, which for me would probably conclude the final week in December. There was going to be a whole lot of traveling between Keizer and Springfield in my future.

Before Betty handed me the 20 page consent form with Jeff Sharman listed as Attending Investigator, she printed my name as Research Participant. She then carefully highlighted page three which clarified the screening procedures before moving on to pages 7-15. These concentrated on the side effects of both drugs, the clinical trial itself, and tests associated with all the necessary procedures. On the top of page 7 I noticed right away the following statement, "There is a rare risk of death." I loved the word 'rare,' but hated the word 'death.'

I'm not a gambler by nature, but I'd been a bit of a risk taker during my long career in education. Besides teaching by day at South Salem High School, I took on the challenge of offering night and summer term college classes at the Oregon State Penitentiary. Better known as the Graybar Hotel, it housed serious male offenders and I was hired to replace a female teacher who had an inappropriate relationship with an inmate and lost her job after being found out. I put myself in jeopardy each time I walked through the metal gates of the prison and I knew that, but precautions were in place for my safety, and I trusted those in charge of it.

During my 15th year at the Graybar something happened though that never could have been prevented. An inmate took it upon himself to "even up the score" because he'd received a 'D' on his previous mid-term exam in my class. Embarrassment, not physical harm, was what David employed when he slid his penis out of the hole he'd torn in the crotch of his Prison Blues and masturbated while sitting in the front row of my night class. Stunned and red in the face, I froze in my chair, only a few feet away from him. He cocked his head to one side, grinned and blew me a kiss while putting his dick back inside his pants. I felt like I'd been beaten up. He'd over-powered and controlled me without even throwing a punch. I wanted to throw up.

Somehow I mustered up enough strength to calmly walk out of my classroom and quickly motion for the duty sergeant. I explained what had happened, and he immediately removed David from class, using the excuse that my student was needed back in his cell. None of David's classmates suspected anything was amiss; they weren't witnesses to his actions, and a student returning to his cell block wasn't anything out of the ordinary. I struggled through to the end of class before going to Sergeant Hansen's office. I thanked him for his help and together we filled out a prison Incident Complaint Form.

The occurrence had to be described in great detail; it would be my word against David's, should he dispute what happened. With the sarge by my side, I wrote exactly what had transpired, down to a description of how big the hole was in his jeans and what his penis looked like- it was uncircumcised with a large flap over the tip and its shaft was dotted with small patches of darkened skin.

Before the following week's class, I learned from the sergeant that inmates didn't tolerate such acts against women, especially their female teachers, and David paid harshly among the inmate population for what he'd done to me. His punishment continued well beyond removal from just my class; he was never allowed to enroll in any others while behind bars at the Oregon State Penitentiary. After that incident, John wanted me to stop teaching at OSP, but I continued in spite of David's actions. I didn't want to quit because I couldn't handle the risks of teaching at The Graybar. I just didn't. And people like Hansen did all they could to help me stay safe and not be hurt again.

What occurred with David many years ago was small compared to the phrase, "Risk of death," on a clinical trial consent form. The idea that something designed to help me live longer could, instead, kill me was terrifying. Part of me felt like sprinting out of the confines of Willamette Valley Cancer Institute and Research Center and driving over to Neskowin to walk its beaches and pretend all this leukemia stuff wasn't really happening. But the bigger part of me knew Sharman, Betty, and all the people I'd seen that day would have my back and control that risk. I gambled on it; like I'd thrown the dice at The Graybar.

John and I wanted a little more information about the cost of the clinical trial and Betty turned to page 17. In summary it stated that the sponsor would provide BG (Bendamustine and Gazyva) at no charge while I participated in the study, and procedures required ONLY for the study and not part of my standard medical care, would also be provided at no cost.

"We have people already in treatment as part of this trial who have the same insurance as yours, and we've had no trouble working with them to receive payments. And costs have been more than reasonable," Betty said.

It was reassuring to hear, but I was no dummy. Those things referred to as "standard medical care" would add up fast toward my $2500 out of pocket maximum. But the cost wasn't going to break the bank, and the trial offered me the longest remission period until I'd have to do another kind of treatment. I figured having more TIME was well worth every penny I was billed.

There's no cure for what I have; **Chronic** Lymphocytic Leukemia is just that, chronic. It keeps coming back and coming back, like a nightmare from childhood you can't get rid of even though as an adult you know monsters aren't real. CLL is masterful at always lurking in the shadows, ruining my peace of mind and never leaving me alone; I worried about the mental toll of the trial.

"I'd like to share something with you," said Betty, bringing me back from my own thoughts.

"Something I think will help you a lot. What I tell all my patients is this: Look at your months on the trial as a part time job, the most important temporary job you'll ever have in your entire life. Don't miss a day of work by doing all you can to stay healthy, follow every direction you're given to the letter, and try your best not to quit before it's finished. When things get tough, we've got you covered, and never ever forget that your health is the most important thing in the world to us."

This lovely woman was completely sincere and there was absolutely no doubt in her eyes. I felt like my risk factors had just gone down. She was one of the guards outside my classroom.

"Thanks," I returned. "Yes, thanks," joined in my husband.

"Any questions?" Betty asked and then added, "Do you want to ask me anything before you drive back home?"

"No. I think that pretty much covers it, for now," I replied. "But can I email or phone you later? I never remember to ask everything I want to know when I'm in a doctor's office. And this is all VERY new to me."

"Sure. I completely understand," said Betty. "Everyone feels that way at the beginning. Here's my card, with my email address and phone number on it. I'll wait to hear from you. Soon, I hope."

We left her office with the oncology research consent form in my grip. The drive back to Keizer was a long and quiet one. We'd taken in so many sights and sounds that morning, exhaustion quickly set in, and we stared silently ahead just like the cancer patients in Sharman's reception room.

Eighty-five minutes later I was rocking gently in the hammock in our backyard. I gazed at a tiny hummingbird sipping sugar water from its feeder and then whizzing across my head to continue a late lunch, flying toward begonias on our covered patio. The sky above was a soft blue, with only a whiff of clouds floating by. I stared at them and the little bird for several minutes, realizing how purely oblivious nature was to my disease and my fear of dying from it. Quickly, part of a D. H. Lawrence poem came to mind.

"I never saw a wild thing sorry for itself.
A small bird will drop frozen dead from a bough
without ever having felt sorry for itself."

My little hummingbird worried nothing about its own mortality, and I envied its carefree existence. Death, and the worry about it, is a human trait. We see ourselves as superior beings on this planet, but our humanity is what keeps us up at night in our never-ending struggle to comprehend and cope with our lives ending before we want them to. Swaying in the hammock with the 20 page clinical consent form, a dictionary, and my favorite pen and highlighter nearby, I first skimmed the document, getting a feel for what it had to say. I read subject headings and especially keyed in on italicized and bold-faced information. My highlighter glided over these, getting my body involved in what my mind was taking in, a time honored technique for remembering what a person reads.

Words and phrases like 'neutropenia,' 'thrombocytopenia,' 'tumor lysis syndrome,' 'progressive multifocal leukoencephalopathy' and 'Steven-Johnson syndrome,' I shaded in light green and then with Webster's help, explained in the margins with my Bic. Next, I slowly and deliberately read every topic and concluding sentence of each paragraph, as well as carefully taking in lists and bulleted information. The document lost its foreign footing and became more and more home grown. Finally, I read with great concentration, every single word on every single page, over and over, oftentimes aloud, to HEAR the content in my own voice. It wasn't a stranger anymore.

After spending three hours in the hammock, my body was covered by the cradle of its rope triangles. I gently tossed my pretty pen and dictionary over on the grass and tried to shift my weight to the side of the hammock. This of course swung it into action and I flipped out, landing with a thud on the sand; luckily the pages of the consent form were stapled together. I escaped my husband's glances, but that same sweet little hummingbird fluttered right in front of my face as if to say, "I saw that coming. Why didn't you?"

Once inside I decided to do something I hadn't considered while reading outside, investigate the company who sponsored the clinical trial. I wanted to find out about the corporate goals of Genentech and get a handle on their values and garner ideas about how they treat both the patients they serve and their own employees. I headed up stairs to visit my computer and typed in Genentech's website, **https://www.gene.com/about-us**. Their mission statement said: "We commit ourselves to scientific rigor, unassailable ethics, and access to medical innovations for all. We do this today to build a better tomorrow." Pretty powerful stuff, but I wasn't going to be won over so easily. I examined their entire site, and then went on to read what other people were saying about Genentech. I tried to find something, anything about them that would repudiate their lovely mission statement. I didn't find a thing.

Returning to the peaceful setting of Johnson's Beach, only this time choosing an Adirondack chair by the fire pit instead of the hammock, I read the whole consent form again. The hummingbird was nowhere to be seen, but a few weeds had shown themselves next to the broccoli in my well tended veggie garden, so I walked over and pulled the invaders up by their roots. Then I strolled by my baby tomatoes and propped up a few of their heavy limbs, and visited my onions and told them how wonderful they looked. Getting my glove-covered hands in the dirt had more and more become one of my basic instincts.

Feeling no longer like a newbie to this whole idea of chemotherapy after a 4th perusal of the forms, I wasn't so consumed with trial fear. In fact, I actually felt a little brave. That's when I turned from thinking only of myself, to thinking and caring about others and about their well being. If I agreed to the trial, I wouldn't be doing it simply for the selfish purpose of moving my expiration date back, but it'd give me the opportunity to advance scientific discovery. Not everybody in life has the chance I held in my hands; the chance to help others who were unknown to me. Maybe they could one day live better and longer lives because of an old grandma who lived in Keizer, a wrinkled broad who liked nothing better than walking the beaches and jumping the waves of Neskowin, Oregon. This could be my small contribution to the larger picture of why any of us are here. And if the trial failed, well that was still helpful. Doctors would know to back up and alter the direction of their research, a crucial step in ultimately achieving success in any medical pursuit.

Still, I had lingering doubts. Did I really want to be a human guinea pig like the other people in Phase I who'd come before me? All those patients could have chosen a more tried and true form of chemo, one that had fewer risk factors when compared to Bendamustine/Gazyva treatment. Their CLL, like mine, hadn't been previously treated so there were many other treatments available, with statistical data to back up success rates. But this trial, and the doctors who believed in it, wanted to bypass the old and try the new, and they needed patients who were willing to do the same. I went back in the house and John asked me if I'd made a decision: to sign or not to sign.

"Yes, I have," was my reply. "It's not going to be easy, but I'm signing."

"I'll be here to help every step of the way; love you, Rabbit," he hugged me with his words.

That is his nickname for me, Rabbit. He'd chosen that term of endearment shortly after we met in 1986. We were snuggled on the couch watching an old black and white movie one night and on TV appeared the classic film, HARVEY, starring Jimmy Stewart. Stewart's best friend is a tall, invisible rabbit; invisible that is to everyone else but Stewart's character, Elwood P. Dowd. By the end of the film, other people also believe in Harvey the rabbit because they WANT to believe. Over the years different nicknames for me have come and gone, but Rabbit has stayed. John's nickname is Squirrel for a lot of reasons, but mostly because we have great affinity for the fast-paced, bushy-tailed woodland creature. We use our names sparingly, reserving them for very special times.

I unstapled page 20 of the consent form, signed and dated it July 22, 2015, and placed it in a stamped envelope addressed to Dr. Jeffrey Sharman at the Willamette Valley Cancer Institute and Research Center. We drove to the nearby post office, dropped it in their mailbox and rewarded ourselves with Starbuck's on the way home.

With the signing of the consent form, I'd become an official candidate for the CLL clinical trial, and had taken the first step in the pre-assessment process. I slept like a baby that night, no bad dreams of crowded lymphocytes jockeying for position in my blood stream, or tubes the size of water hoses squirting drugs into my veins. These I might have expected, but I didn't dream at all; my sleep was peaceful and without any scary interruptions.

Waiting for Betty to pick up her phone the next morning though, a sudden flash of the crazy dream I had the night after having my breasts cut off quickly circulated in my memory. In the dream I was floating in the air above the table where a pathologist carved my sweet bosoms into tiny pieces, like a skilled butcher slicing thin strips of salami. I tried desperately to get the man's attention to stop his mutilation of my breasts, but the Helen Reddy song, "I Am Woman," was booming so loudly in the background he'd put in earplugs to drown out the lyrics. It was no wonder he couldn't hear my pleas.

Betty answered just as her phone was ready to take a message, and she was more than happy I'd consented to join the trial and had mailed in the paperwork. After a few pleasantries, she asked me if I'd recently seen my dentist. "It's important you have a clean bill of health regarding oral care before starting any kind of treatment."

"Had my teeth cleaned and X-rayed last month. Everything's in good shape. No cavities or anything, and Dr Fromherz did a cancer screening too, so everything's fine." I paused and then added, "At least with my teeth."

"Great! And how about flu and pneumonia shots; all up-to-date?"

"Yep. Got a flu shot last fall and had both the PCV 13 and PPSV23 vaccines months ago. Dr. Strother told me the shots might not be as effective because of my CLL, but to make sure I got them anyway. Better to have a little protection than none at all. Oh, and he reminded me again NOT to get a shingles shot because that vaccine contains a live virus, the kind my body can't handle like it used to."

"Good to hear. You've done all the right things," she said in a motherly fashion. "The next step is to get you back here as soon as we can. We need to make sure we've got your complete health history, draw all the blood required for pre-treatment tests, arrange an EKG and get a CT scan of your neck and abdomen. Oh, and a BMA, a bone marrow aspiration, by Sharman."

"How do I go about all that?" I questioned her.

"Don't worry, Pam. I'll make all the arrangements. We just have to decide on a date and time. You're from out of town, so how about if we try and do everything in one day?"

"Isn't that a lot all at once?" I responded.

"No. Not really. It's not unusual, and patients seem to cope with the tests just fine," Betty reassured me. "But we could divvy things up if you'd rather."

I hesitated a few seconds and then said, "Let's get everything over in one day. If other patients have done it, then I guess I can too. Just give me at least enough time to find out about my most recent Merkel antibody test results, have my dermatologist check out a spot on my lower leg and bring my internist Dr. Wang and my Salem oncologist, Dr. Strother, up to speed. Okay?"

"Absolutely," Betty responded. "How long will those things take, do you think?"

"No more than a week. Sent my blood to Seattle 10 days ago, so I'll be hearing from their lab anytime now, and I see my dermatologist tomorrow. I'll email you with those results and if everything's 'a go' I'll contact Wang and Strother."

"Fine. Once I hear back from you, I'll call scheduling and we'll get things on the books. Any questions?"

"Nope," I answered more casually than I felt. We quickly said our good-byes and in a few minutes I was at the computer scanning my email for blood results of my most recent Merkel antibody tests from Dr. Nghiem's lab at the University of Washington. I relaxed when I read that I remained in the negative range of <74, always great news that to this day I never take for granted.

After a visit with Dr. Hale the following morning, the lesion on my leg was diagnosed as seborrheic keratosis, a benign skin condition. Since I was already no spring chicken, I'd have more and more ugly spots to look forward to with each birthday celebration. Ugliness aside, I was very thankful my growth was no more than an appearance issue. This body had enough on her mind with the clinical trial looming in the months ahead without another kind of skin cancer.

I emailed Betty that same afternoon and told her the good news, both parts of it. My Merkel tests were negative, and my skin problem was nothing to worry about. Things could move forward.

Just two days later, a long email from her arrived explaining all the tests we'd discussed earlier and requested from me a confirmation of the date and time of August 4th, 9:00 am. She'd even typed in caps and bold print that I had to fast prior to my arrival because of my early morning CT scan. She ended her email by telling me she had already contacted Salem Hospital and scheduled my Port insertion for Monday, August 10th, at noon. "Good grief!" I told my computer. "This girl is both fast AND efficient!"

To equal Betty's speed, I phoned her and we confirmed the August 4th pre-assessment appointment and tests. All was ready, except my mental state. I badly needed a crash course in fighting jitters. So I turned to my grandkids, spending lots and lots of time with them. Even though we'd recently returned from our seven day family vacation in Neskowin, I craved more of the joy and happiness of being around Sydney and Aiden. They, more than anyone else in my life, possess the power to make me forget my ailments and any attempts at their control.

We spent hours doing kid stuff and I forgot all about CLL. We found new places for hide and seek; we played endless soccer in the backyard and cheered on the Portland Timbers when we wanted a break in our own game. We went on bike rides up to Baskin Robbins and got cones of Rocky Road and Mint Chocolate Chip, we went swimming and rock climbing at the Kroc Center, we hit tennis balls at the Courthouse, and more than anything, we just 'hung out' together, taking in each other's company. Sydney and Aiden were exactly what Grandma needed as the days crawled toward August 4th. Finally, when it arrived I felt as ready as I'd ever be.

The temperature was already in the low 80's as we drove to Springfield. Drops of sweat dotted my forehead and upper lip and perspiration wetted my armpits. All the H2O wasn't just from the weather; I was scared beyond simple jitters as the trials of the trial stared me smack in the face.

"You ok?" queried my perceptive husband.

"Thought I was ready, but maybe I'm not."

"Just say the word and I'll turn this car around," John said, giving me an out.

I slowed my breathing, took in the cool air of the car and drank some water. As the outside world sped by, I noticed a Red Tail hawk balanced on a fence post, his keen eyes searching a farmer's field for a tender morsel of mouse. I looked in my rearview mirror and spied him again as he launched himself low over his domain, swoop down and catch a small creature in his talons and fly off in the distance.

"I'll be alright," I said. "Not great, but alright for now and when I get there I'll be ready."

As usual we arrived 15 minutes early, just enough time to talk with Gretchen who answered insurance questions and had printed out a copy of my Estimated Patient Treatment Summary. Pre-meds, Bendamustine and Gazyva, and a Neulasta shot were listed as $4,446.20 and with my Patient Coinsurance Percentage of 20%, my share was $888.20.

"This must be the **total** cost for August, right?" I asked naively.

"Nooooooo," she extended her reply. "This is just the first treatment in August."

My sick sense of humor right away kicked into gear and I came back with, "Shit, it's a hell of a lot cheaper to die! My cremation plan is all paid up. Keizer Funeral Parlor will pick up my corpse, shove it into their oven, and then my ashes can be retrieved once they've cooled." The nice insurance lady looked horrified and my husband let out a tiny gasp.

My sweet, level-headed John reminded me that our out of pocket maximum co-pay was $2500 for the ENTIRE year; that's all we'd be responsible for. That was great and probably just pocket-change for the top 1% of the US of A, but half of $5,000 was still a whole lot of greenbacks for us Johnsons.

The reality is health care costs in our country are outrageous and a single-payer system is demonized as socialism. The rich and well off receive better care than those of us who struggle to pay our bills; it's unfair, unethical, and unchristian. Wishing I had a nitro to place under my tongue, Gretchen said the bill was only a preliminary agreement and assured us it would go down significantly, especially since I was part of a clinical trial. She handed me a copy after I grudgingly signed the estimate. No wonder people were going bankrupt trying to pay doctor bills and there were so many GoFundMe sites on the internet. I didn't zing the insurance lady with another of my tirades; after all, she was just the messenger, not the policy maker of our nation's health care system.

Betty soon called us back to an exam room, and first I met with Dr. Sharman who gave me a thorough once over, taking special note of my ever expanding spleen and swollen lymph nodes. "Nothing unusual for CLL patients," he said politely when our eyes met. And then he continued with, "How are you feeling otherwise, Pam?"

"Really not too bad," I answered. "Maybe a little more tired than usual, but no real fatigue that's kept me from doing what I usually do."

"No night sweats, fevers, infections?" he questioned.

"No. None at all."

"Good. Very good," he said. "Well, you know today is a busy day for you both," he shared a smile with my hubby. "You'll be answering some questions for Betty, then we'll do a blood draw and EKG, and send you over to Oregon Imaging for your CT scan. After that you'll have about an hour or so break to get something to eat before I see you again for your BMA. I'll be numbing you up real good so you'll hardly feel a thing, except for some pressure and maybe five seconds of sharp pain. It'll be over before you know it."

"Sounds good," I stated with confidence, and with that he was gone and Betty fired questions at me about the complete medical history I'd already faxed to their office. She re-affirmed my list of medications, my dental clearance, checked about any surgeries I might have forgotten to include and was especially careful about double checking my allergy to statins, and confirming I'd fasted at least four hours for my CT scan. I felt like an astronaut buckled in the seat of my capsule, doing a system's countdown before take- off.

Becky then had me step on the scales one more time because my weight would be an important determining factor in getting the correct dosage of drugs during the clinic trial. At 5'9"and hefty, my dosage would be drastically different than some 5'2" petite waif who looked like she'd never eaten a Burger King Whopper in her life. Not that I eat **that** often at the joint with the crowns.

Next, she hooked me up for an electrocardiogram. "You know, I've had a few of these, but never really understood what they were for," I mentioned.

"It's pretty straightforward," she responded. "An electrocardiogram, sometimes referred to as an EKG or ECG, is a simple test that detects and records your heart's electrical activity. It can show how your heart is beating, whether the rhythm of your heartbeats is steady or irregular, and the strength and timing of the electrical impulses passing through each part of your heart."

She showed John and me 1 of the 10 electrodes she'd be placing on my chest, arms and legs. "A little like Bride of Frankenstein, don't you think?" I kidded.

"A bit," she laughed. "This won't take long." And she was right. Within 5 minutes all 10 were correctly placed and the machine did its job of recording the beats of my heart. In a flash Betty removed the EKG stickers and said everything looked completely normal. "No irregularities found, whatsoever," were her exact words.

She then escorted me, alone, to the lab for a draw that filled 17 vials, breaking my previous individual record set at the Seattle Cancer Care Alliance when I totaled 15 for Nghiem's study of Merkel antibodies. My arm and hand were nice and warm thanks to the phlebotomist's preparations, and the purple colored blood ran smoothly and without interruption into the containers, even while a fire alarm sounded for all of us to exit the building. A nurse wanted us to stop the draw and follow correct protocol, but we were on vial number 12 and Betty said we were going to stay our ground and finish the job so I didn't have to endure another poke. A minute later we headed for the nearby stairway inside the treatment room, a safe place while the alarm still sounded. We sat close to one another and she looked at me with great concern.

"Let's sit here for while," she said. "You've given too much blood to have to hurry to the elevator, go down five floors and then walk from the parking lot to across the street. It's only a drill and we shouldn't have to abide by rules if it means putting a patient's safety in jeopardy."

"I don't want to get you in trouble," I worried as my face got paler.

"You won't. There was a slight pause and grin on her part before she continued, "Sharman would back us up all the way and what he says goes a long way around here."

We waited a few more minutes until my color returned, my clammy hands dried and the all clear bell signaled the fire drill was over. "Guess I'll head to the lobby and then John and I will go to Oregon Imaging now, right?"

"Yes. They're expecting you. Remember, when you're finished there, you and your husband can grab a bite to eat, but then be back here again at 12:20 for your BMA."

John and I left and made good time driving the short distance to Eugene and Oregon Imaging. My CT scan went without a hitch, the contrasting dye flowing through my body with no adverse reactions and a skilled technician moving me in and out of the machine like she'd done it a million times before.

The scans zeroed in on my neck and abdomen areas, and I knew from my reading of the consent form that they'd eventually be compared to post-treatment scans. If they didn't show improvement, if blood tests didn't indicate lower levels of lymphocytes and better WBC counts, then the clinical trial hadn't done what we all hoped it would do. Pre-assessments and post-assessments were crucial to determining the success of combining Bendamustine and Gazyva. I'd signed on for this sixth month part time job and I was going to be the best "employee" possible, so it was time to eat and ease into this whole BMA thing.

"How'd it go?" my hubby asked as I joined him in the waiting room.

"A piece of cake," was my immediate reply. "Any ideas where we can get a sandwich? Don't exactly feel like eating a lot, but I can tell I need something."

"Well, how do you feel about eating at Subway?" he asked.

"Maybe we could get a Subway and take it somewhere and eat. Just you and me, without any other people around. And outside, can we eat outside?"

"Absolutely, whatever you want, Rabbit."

We drove back into Springfield and got subs, lemonade, and a chocolate chip cookie at the Gateway Mall near WVCI and Sharman's office. John then drove to a tiny park where we slowly ate our lunch under the shade of an old oak tree, its huge roots bulging up from the grass. It was now well over 90 degrees. I traded off between drinking my bottled water and over sweetened lemonade, while taking a few pathetic bites of my six inch teriyaki chicken on wheat. I only nibbled at my cookie, very out of character for me. A good appetite was something I'd definitely left at home and John wasn't eating great either.

"You know, I can remember coming here as a kid," he said. "My friends and I used to ride bikes along the cement path all around the park. And we'd pop wheelies to see who could do the best ones. We'd stay here as long as we could until we figured our folks would start worrying about us."

"Ever think you'd be lying on a blanket here with your wife some day? Or maybe I should say, ever think someday you'd get laid by a divorcee 10 years older than you who's on her third cancer?"

He laughed and answered, "Wouldn't have it any other way. Pinkie swear."

Our pinkie swear was and always has been sacred. It means that whatever is said to one another or to another person is the truth, the whole truth and nothing but the truth. For us, following up with a pinkie swear is a stronger commitment to truth than the putting of a hand on a Bible in a court of law. A pinkie swear can't be requested as verification of something; it has to be given freely by the one making the swear. John REALLY was glad to be lying on the blanket with me, just as I was with him. "Sorry about all this," I stated.

"It's not your fault. You gotta know this is NOT your fault," he took my hand.

"I know. It's just that sometimes I want to apologize. Makes me feel a little better about all this mess of cancer." I choked back the big lump in my throat, held his hand tighter, and then went on. "Your life's been fouled up by it so often and the Big C has taken away your smile way too many times. I want to take care of you; not the other way around."

John smiled, pulled me close and kissed my forehead. "Everything's going to be okay. You NEVER have to apologize for anything that's not your fault."

We finished what we could of our lunch and made our way to Sharman's office. It was noon.

I checked in at reception and we began the wait for my procedure. Outside, the rolling hills of Springfield were a light brown, sad and longing for the rains of an Oregon fall, winter, and spring. Yes, we get a lot of rain, and I mean a lot, buckets and buckets of rain. But the trade off is gorgeous summers and an environment so clean and pure that people want to move here...and stay.

Outside, I saw the old horse in her usual spot, gnawing on some green alfalfa before strolling over to drink from her metal trough. The puzzle on the round table was complete except for two missing pieces right in the middle of another Monet masterpiece. I worked to find my "center," to calm myself with the probability that worry about a bone marrow aspiration was most likely worse than the reality of it. Most things in my life had played out that way.

"Pam, Dr. Sharman is ready for you," said Betty as she walked toward us. John wanted to accompany me, but I wouldn't let him. Watching long needles being stuck in my back was a thing I insisted on doing alone, not with him by my side sharing my pain.

"It'll be alright, Sweetie," I told him. "Be back in no time. I got this."

I followed Betty to the exam room and the calm I worked for set in. Betty checked my blood pressure and heart rate as I watched a nurse prepare slides, instruments, and large needles on the counter next to the sink. Dr. Sharman joined our threesome and slowly explained the whole procedure.

He said he'd select a spot in my lower back hip area, clean and mark it and then numb it well. Next, he would make a small incision and insert a hollow needle through the bone and into the bone marrow. Using a syringe attached to the needle, he would withdraw a sample of the liquid portion of the marrow. He said to expect a brief sharp pain or stinging for about 5-10 seconds, with the entire aspiration taking a few minutes.

"He uses a lot of numbing medicine so his patients hardly feel a thing," Betty said, offering reassurance. "You'll do fine, Pam."

"You can lay on your side or your chest," said Sharman. "Whatever feels most comfortable."

I first tried my left side and then switched to my stomach, placing my head on my arms which I'd crossed under my chin. "Wish this was a massage table," I thought to myself. "Then I could rest my head in the table's face hole and solve all my comfort issues." Finally, I settled in and took a deep breath. "You alright?" asked Betty. "Yes, I'm fine," I lied.

The nurse came over and pulled down my slacks and panties a little so Sharman could get at my hip area, then she covered my exposed backside with a paper sheet. Betty rubbed my shoulders and neck and I relaxed, forcing my mind to walk down every street in Neskowin and gaze at all the old, pretty, quaint cottages. Their yards always overflowed with sweet peas and roses, bachelor buttons and hydrangeas, and Oregon coral found on the beach close to Proposal Rock. I fantasized about which cottage we would buy some day and how we'd enjoy the beach each morning, picking up floats and driftwood and sand dollars. Then came Dr. Sharman's intrusion.

"I'm going to press on your hip area to find the spot I want to go in, okay?"

"Sure," I answered. Betty rubbed faster, and I day dreamed harder.

"This is it," I heard Sharman say. "This is the spot." He marked his incision point. "I'll deaden this area and then I'll proceed. It will be real quick and over before you know it."

"That's what she said," slipped out of my mouth and apparently no one in the room was a diehard fan of the TV series, THE OFFICE, because I didn't even get a soft chuckle.

"Here we go," stated Sharman.

I closed my eyes and took myself far away from where I was.

"Doing okay, Pam?" asked Betty.

"Yes," I answered; this time telling the truth.

I felt the pressure of the hollow needle, but no real pain. When Dr. Sharman reached the hip bone, Betty told me to take a deep breath and then hold it for a few seconds. I followed her directions to the letter and experienced deeper pressure, but no real sharpness or stinging. Fluid was quickly collected and examined under a microscope with me still on the table. It was double checked to make sure enough had been drawn and the selection provided the right type of marrow fluid for proper cell testing. Sharman had hit a home run.

He then pulled out the hollow needle and put a gauze compression bandage over the incision site. His nurse pressed on it for a few minutes to prevent any bleeding. Betty continued rubbing my shoulders and telling me what a good patient I'd been. It was over, at least the first bone marrow aspiration. The nurse then removed the compression bandage and exchanged it for a regular band aid. She and Betty had me turn over on my back and stay that way for 20 minutes before I was finally allowed to return to the reception area. Squirrel greeted me with a relieved look on his face and I said, "Let's go home."

"Remember, your port insertion for treatment is Monday, the 10th, at Salem Hospital," mentioned Betty as she followed us to the elevator. "I'm sure it will go well."

"Thanks for the wonderful backrub," I told her, as John looked at me quizzically. "Wish you could be there for the port."

"You'll be sound asleep and won't feel a thing. Most of our chemo patients love their ports because it's so much easier to infuse drugs than constantly poking around your arm or hand for good veins," Betty reminded me.

"I've been meaning to ask you," I added, "What if all these tests indicate I'm not accepted into the trial? Do I still get the port inserted on Monday?"

"Yes," said Betty, and then she continued, "I'll contact you before then if any problems arise with your tests to prevent your acceptance. Try not to worry."

We reached the elevator and disappeared behind its closed doors. While staring at the control panel as we changed floors, I wondered why Betty had said **most** but not all chemo patients loved their ports. I immediately chose "not to go there" any further, to stop worrying, to abandon the "dis-ease" of my disease. If I could control the worry over my CLL for the five days before my port insertion, the time could be mine and not the minefield of leukemia.

With great effort on my part and the help of those around me, I left the world of cancer and enjoyed to the fullest my time before my chest port and start of chemo. Each day was glorious! John and I walked the dog park at Minto Island in South Salem a few times and petted every canine that wandered our way, especially the golden retrievers. At night we watched silly, funny comedies like Christopher Guest's WAITING FOR GUFFMAN and BEST IN SHOW, the Marx Brothers, Abbott and Costello classics, SNL and our favorite OFFICE episodes. We spent an entire day at Neskowin taking in her beautiful beaches, napping on the soft sand and eating lunch at the Hawk Creek Café. We took Syd and Aiden to River Road Park one afternoon, and then later their parents, our daughter Karin and her husband Drew, had us over for a bar-b-que and soccer in their huge backyard. We walked to McNary High School one morning where I'd graduated in 1966 and played tennis, afterwards leaving our can of new balls for some beginners on the next court. Another morning we drove to Keizer Nursery and bought tulip and daffodil bulbs to border my vegetable beds and another day we went to EZ Orchards for local sweet corn, chocolate covered filberts and marionberry syrup.

During those days I finished the second reading of EINSTEIN by Walter Isaacson; I had a yearning to **really** understand one of the most basic principles in the world, 'The Theory of Relativity. ' And again I went through THE COMPLETE COLLECTED POEMS of MAYA ANGELOU, with special enjoyment of her feminist masterpiece, 'Phenomenal Woman.' The words danced on the page and covered me in the joy of just being myself.

PHENOMENAL WOMAN

Pretty women wonder where my secret lies.
I'm not cute or built to suit a fashion model's size
But when I start to tell them,
They think I'm telling lies.
I say,
It's in the reach of my arms
The span of my hips,
The stride of my step,
The curl of my lips.
I'm a woman
Phenomenally.
Phenomenal woman,

That's me.

I walk into a room

Just as cool as you please,

And to a man,

The fellows stand or

Fall down on their knees.

Then they swarm around me,

A hive of honey bees.

I say,

It's the fire in my eyes,

And the flash of my teeth,

The swing in my waist,

And the joy in my feet.

I'm a woman

Phenomenally.

Phenomenal woman,

That's me.

Men themselves have wondered

What they see in me.

They try so much

But they can't touch

My inner mystery.

When I try to show them,

They say they still can't see.

I say,

It's in the arch of my back,

The sun of my smile,

The ride of my breasts,

The grace of my style.

I'm a woman

Phenomenally
Phenomenal woman,
That's me.

Now you understand
Just why my head's not bowed.
I don't shout or jump about
Or have to talk real loud.
When you see me passing,
It ought to make you proud.
I say,
It's in the click of my heels,
The bend of my hair,
the palm of my hand,
The need for my care.
'Cause I'm a woman
Phenomenally.
Phenomenal woman,
That's me.

Besides the reading of great literature, on more than one occasion during those five precious days I threw caution to the wind and let old Charlie cat sleep at the foot of my bed where he enjoyed the air conditioning much more than the August temperatures in the garage. He had become my comfort animal at home, while my old horse was my comfort where I "worked."

A much anticipated email arrived from Betty one afternoon during our vacation from CLL. She told me I'd "Passed" the pre-assessment tests and she would order my Benda and Obinutuzumab (Gazyva) the day before I started treatment. She put in two prescriptions at my Safeway Pharmacy; one was Compazine for nausea and the other was Allopurinol which would help protect me from Tumor Lysis Syndrome, one of the most serious side-effects of the trial. The syndrome occurs when huge numbers of cancer cells die all at once and then join together to form tumors. It's these tumors that can release their contents into a patient's bloodstream, causing death; Allopurinal is meant to prevent that life-threatening event during early infusions.

Betty instructed me to start the Allopurinol on Sunday, the day before my port procedure, and keep taking it for the following three days. She also advised me to pick up some generic Claritin and Ibuprofen to keep on hand should I encounter any bone pain as a result of treatment.

Finally, she finished the email with a reminder to get my port placed Monday at Salem Hospital as planned, and then came the statement, "Tracy RN will be taking over your research nursing care for the treatment portion of your trial." Betty had gotten me ready for the trial and done this with great skill and gentleness; now I'd be counting on a nurse called Tracy to get me across the finish line of six months of chemotherapy.

John and I arrived at Salem Hospital on Monday at noon for my port. I'd done my due diligence and read up on the procedure and knew pretty well what to expect. With an IV deftly inserted in my left arm and blood pressure and temperature normal, we waited patiently in pre-op room # 16, one away from my lucky number.

Dr. Stack, who was as easy on the eyes as Dr. Sharman, entered with a small triangle- shaped port in hand and showed me where it'd be inserted in my chest. He also briefly explained how the whole Power Port with Groshong Catheter worked. "Wow, no more arm pokes!" I marveled.

A couple of minutes later an anesthesiologist arrived all decked out in blue scrubs and checked my chart for allergies to medications then assured me I'd be comfortable during the procedure and back in my room in no time at all. With enthusiasm running high and no doubts about a successful implantation, I closed my eyes to block out the glaring hospital lights and almost fell asleep.

"Doing okay?" asked my loving husband.

"Yep," I answered. "Just hate those darn bright lights. Always have and always will."

Before he turned the switches off, a nurse, also in her scrubs, came in and said it was time to go. She made sure my IV machine was disconnected from the wall and told John I'd be back soon. He kissed me on the forehand and I rolled down the hallway to a small, VERY cold operating room. There I slid onto another table and then was politely introduced to the team who would be assisting Dr. Stack. The anesthesiologist, who was already at my side, put a little something in my IV line and I got woozy.

When Stack appeared, things really started happening. My chest was cleaned and prepped, instruments were placed on a roll cart and moved next to me, the giant disk surgical light overhead was tilted at the perfect angle and people in the room checked off their tasks in preparation for what was about to begin. The last thing I remember was watching tiny droplets of blood dirtying the snow white cloth draped over my face and hearing someone say, "Let's put her under."

Back in #16, I woke up quickly and felt fine. The left side of my chest sported a small raised area under my skin where the port had been inserted, but I was in no pain. A few minutes later the doc came in to check on me and tell us that everything had gone great. He explained that the little bump was called a "reservoir," the part where a needle would be inserted to give my chemo drugs or draw blood whenever I needed it. He also explained that the catheter was a thin, flexible tube that extended from the reservoir itself and was placed into a large vein. "The whole thing is designed for people like you whose other veins are difficult to access by usual means," he clarified. Needless to say, I liked the sound of that.

By 2:00 o'clock I was discharged, but only after a nurse explained the serious warning signs to watch for regarding an infection at my incision site. Signs were a bad smell, swelling, redness or excessive drainage, increasing pain in the area of my port and a fever which wouldn't improve with over-the-counter medicine. We drove home and I climbed into my wonderful bed and slept blissfully, avoiding my left side. Waking around 5:00pm, I took my second Allopurinol and was back in bed by 8:00 o'clock. The port insertion had taken more out of me than I thought it would.

Tuesday we took our two mile walk around the neighborhood about mid-morning and then welcomed the grandkids after lunch for a play date. I could tell they'd been coached by their parents not to rough house in any way, shape or form with grandma, and to be on their best behavior, which I'm happy to say is never out of the ordinary for either of them.

We played on Johnson's Beach once more, digging a big hole in the middle. Then we covered the bottom with extra strength, 30 gallon garbage bags and hosed in water to fill our "lake." We had great fun adding agates and seashells along its banks and planting stalks of celery from my veggie garden to mimic palm trees. When we tired of that adventure, we went inside for snack plates of sliced Honey Crisp apples, Pirate Booty Baked Rice and Corn Puffs, mango fruit leather, vanilla yogurt, Tillamook cheese squares and bagels. All this was downed with apple juice, followed by a treat of thin, mint filled Oreos. Having a variety of food choices is always a big deal at our house.

We spent the next hour or so cuddled together watching Tom and Jerry cartoons, an episode each of Dog with a Blog and Wonder Woman, and then rounded out our play date with making paper airplanes and Syd winning at the board game, Sorry. By 3:00 in the afternoon Karin and Drew picked the kiddos up and hustled them home, making sure I got rest before starting chemo early the next morning.

As our family drove away John and I stood on the porch and waved to the grandkids, our fingers making the deaf sign for LOVE. It was a tradition we started when they were babies and they always returned to us. Tomorrow was the big day; part of me looked forward to killing those damn lymphocytes and part of me, the little girl part of me, wanted to hide under my bed, close my eyes and be whisked off to OZ.

AWFUL AUGUST

I wish I could say that the first month of chemo was a cinch and that I sailed through it with flying colors. I wish I could say there were no glitches in the system, no drugs had bad side-effects, no vomit ever missed the toilet, and I didn't think for a minute that the whole trial thing was too much for this senior citizen. But these would be lies, damnable lies of monumental proportion.

For me, day 1 of cycle 1 of the Phase II CLL Clinical Trial which combined Bendamustine and Gazyva among over 100 patients in the United States began on Wednesday, August 12, 2015, at 7:30 am. My memory of that particular day is crystal clear, all the minute details pounded into me, just like my remembrances of JFK's assassination and the crumbling of the Twin Towers; and the look back at the birth of my only child Karin and the entrance into this world of my precious grandchildren. Some memories are cloaked in sadness, and others in joy, but no matter the emotional responses they elicit, they are forever powerful and with little effort are pulled from the past and made present.

John and I arrived at WVCI that morning to a lobby void of other patients. Maybe it was the early hour, or maybe everyone was in with their doctors or already populating the treatment area. Anyway, it seemed unusual for such a busy place to be empty except for us and the people behind the reception desk. Soon my name was called by a phlebotomist I hadn't seen before, and back I went to the lab expecting an easy draw from my wonderful Power Port, placed days earlier by Dr. Stack. Wrong!

Dr. Sharman had requested the draw be from my arm, so, according to the technician, "a more accurate test result could be attained prior to starting treatment for the first time." I complied, but I sure wasn't happy about it. Fortunately though, as the last vial was being capped and labeled and cotton ball and flexible wrap covered my needle site, Betty walked in with Tracy. My new clinical trial nurse was pretty, just like Betty, but much taller, around six feet or close to it. And as Tracy came forward to shake my hand I noticed right away that she moved like an athlete, self-assured and comfortable in her own body. Her smile was warm and so was her greeting.

"Hi, Pam. It's good to finally meet you in person. I've been reading your file and Betty's brought me up to speed on your whole health history. Sorry you've had to go through so much over the years."

"Well, the good news is I'm still here," I replied, grinning as I removed myself from the lab chair. We went to the lobby and got John, and all four of us headed to Sharman's office, with my nurses leading the way.

Watching Tracy's stride and loose movement at the hips and shoulders I guessed she might have been a basketball player in her day, maybe a great high school forward or solid member of a college team. I'd always been intrigued by how people walked; knowing that everyone has a highly individual way of moving, similar to the uniqueness of our one of a kind set of fingerprints.

When my first husband and I taught and coached track at McKenzie High School, about 40 miles east of Eugene, part of our recruitment strategy was indiscreetly following students as they walked the hallways. If kids mostly walked on the front part of their feet and bounced as they took each stride and were slightly toed in, we'd consider them sprinters, 400 meter relay members, hurdlers, and long jumpers. If other kids were tall and gangly, their big feet pointing forward with a touch of spring in their size 12's, then most likely they'd find success as high jumpers. Students with long strides and more heel-to-toe foot placement, they were definitely the ones selected for greater distances such as the half mile, mile and beyond. My ex and I didn't have everything down to a precise science, but we had our share of McKenzie Eagles going on to compete in state track meets.

Inside Sharman's office, Betty checked to make sure I'd been taking the Allopurinol as directed, especially that morning's dosage and also NOT to take it tomorrow or Friday. She said on those two days, Bendamustine was going to be part of my treatment and Benda, in combination with Allopurinol, could significantly increase my risk for a serious rash and fever. Next, she handed me a treatment calendar for August 2015, through February 2016, which made clear on which days I would be having Bendamustine and Gazyva, my labs, a visit with Sharman or his PA, Pat, a detailed health questionnaire to check on my well-being, post-assessment tests and procedures and most importantly, when I'd receive either a Neulasta shot or patch.

Neulasta wasn't a required part of the clinical trial so I'd need to pick up any cost not covered by my own insurance, but adding it to my treatment regime would greatly reduce my risk of infection for the next six months while my white blood cells were bombarded with chemo. I'd seen plenty of commercials on TV about the effectiveness of Neulasta and done thorough research on it so had already decided the extra safety it afforded me was a wise decision. The calendar indicated Neulasta was needed on August 15, September 11, October 9, November 6 and December 4 and 30. Those dates were carefully planned to follow my treatment days, which usually were two per month, with the exception of August when I'd endure five chemo sessions. The plan was to eradicate those mutated and immortal lymphocytes ASAP!

While Betty, Tracy, John and I waited together for Sharman, I filled out my first health questionnaire. It contained questions like; "Are your daily activities limited?" "Are you short of breath?" "Do you feel nauseated or constipated?" "Do you worry and feel depressed?" Answers to such topics fell into four categories; Not at All, A Little, Quite a Bit, and Very Much. Also, some of the 46 questions had to do with me judging my quality of life on a scale of one being very poor and seven being excellent. Needless to say I didn't circle seven. Betty told me to turn the three page questionnaire over to Tracy just as a nurse arrived to take my temperature, blood pressure and pulse. All were within normal range. With my folder of info in hand, Tracy double-checked my records for which medications I was on. The baton of my care had definitely been passed forward.

"Once a day I take Paxil, 20 mg; Zyrtex, 10 mg; B12, 1000 mcg; and D3, 4000 mcg. Think that's it," I replied.

"So you've stopped the Lipitor?" Tracy asked.

"Yes. A while ago because of persistent bone pain."

"And you're aware that Neulasta might cause bone and joint pain too? And that Claritin and Ibuprofen can give you some relief?" continued Tracy.

"Yes."

"If you haven't already got those things at home I can get them for you at our pharmacy today," she offered.

"No, that's okay. I got some a couple days ago. But thanks anyway."

She smiled and made a note of something in my file. "We'll be getting your blood results from your draw real soon," she stated while checking her watch.

"If it's alright, I'd like copies of all my blood tests each time I'm here," I said.

"Absolutely. I'll make copies of all your tests and all your procedures. Would you like me to send copies to your Internist in Salem, Dr. Wang, as well as your local oncologist, Dr. Strother?"

"That'd be great," I answered, very impressed by the fact she already knew the other doctors mentioned in my case file. My clinical trial nurses were more than on the ball, they carried the ball.

Sharman hurried in, looked me straight in the eye and said my neutrophils, RBC, platelets and other key results were good for me to start chemo that day, but apparently there was a little problem.

"Darn, darn, double darn!" I said to myself. Being the consummate planner that I am, I never liked hearing about unexpected health situations that included problems, no matter their size. Having toxic chemicals flow through my veins and a consent form that included *risk of death* as a possibility, was enough already.

It was made clear to me that because I'd had the port inserted outside of Willamette Valley Cancer Institute and Research Center, I needed its placement checked with Dr. Stack at Salem Hospital. "We're trying to reach him right now," said Sharman. "We have specific guidelines here and want to make sure theirs are approved by us. The catheter runs close to your heart and we just want to make sure everything's going to be okay."

"That doesn't exactly sound like a little problem," expressed my worried husband.

"We want a picture of the port/catheter placement and then we'll move ahead with things," stated Sharman. "Really, it's nothing to be overly concerned about. Things will be resolved soon. In the meantime, I think you should go over to the treatment area and get settled in."

Tracy and Betty looked over at John and me for our approval. "Maybe that's the only glitch for today," I said hopefully.

The ladies smiled and took us across reception and into the large treatment room. It was a little after 8:00 am when I sat down in the tan recliner with the 'Reserved' sign on its back. No patients were seated on either side. Tracy moved close and asked if I wanted something to drink, like apple juice or water.

"We've come pretty prepared," grinned John. He'd been carrying my small Neskowin beach bag full of past CLL records, fresh fruit, protein bars, a couple of raisin bagels, baggies of wheat thins and pretzels and two bottles of water. Also stuffed inside was my old iPad, knitting, and a deck of cards.

"We probably brought way too much," he added, as Betty and Tracy watched him carefully unload all our necessities and ready them for my first day of chemo.

"It's going to be a long one. I think you've done exactly what you should do," complimented Tracy.

"I'll make those copies of your blood tests and be right back," said

Betty. She quickly left the treatment room for her office, and we continued waiting for word about the port placement. Tracy stayed by our side telling us about the pre-meds I'd be taking to help me better handle the chemo. Things like Tylenol, Benadryl, anti-nausea drugs, and others would be administered before treatment began. She went on to say that today only Gazyva was being given, but the drug's very common side-effects were nausea, fever, chills, itching or rash, low blood pressure, vomiting, rapid heart rate, sensation of throat or tongue swelling, and shortness of breath. I'd read about all these and others in the consent form, but they sounded much more ominous now.

"What in the hell have I gotten into?" I asked myself. I grabbed one of the water bottles and downed a couple quick gulps.

"I know what you're thinking," said Tracy. "If you experience any of these side-effects, we'll stop Gazyva immediately and take care of you. Most patients have one or two adverse reactions at about 9 minutes into treatment, and that's when we stop. Only after they've passed and you start feeling better will we resume the chemo. Fortunately, such effects never occur again.

"Never?" I questioned with doubt in my voice.

"Almost never, ever," she honestly came back. "Very rarely, VERY," she emphasized.

"I'll take you at your word; almost never and very rarely." I took another big swig of water and rocked out of the recliner and reached into my purse for Sydney and Aiden's school pictures and placed them on the windowsill in front of me. Each kiddo stared back with big smiles on their faces; looking at them every day of treatment would be a constant reminder of what I had awaiting me at home. Outside, the old horse stood in the field across the street and looked my way, a big chunk of hay in her mouth. She chewed slowly, like a cow gnawing on its cud.

I noticed that some people had used colored window markers to share their own or favorite quotes with others in the treatment room. One saying was written all in red caps and by Eleanor Roosevelt, "A woman is like a tea bag- you never know how strong she is until she gets in hot water." Without a doubt, the hot water I was in right now would definitely test my mettle. I just hoped and prayed I'd be strong enough for the task that lie ahead of me, and when tested, rise to the occasion.

Beneath Eleanor's words and written in graceful cursive, was another message, only this time authored by Maya Angelou. It said, "Life is not measured by the number of breaths we take, but by the moments that take our breath away." Yes, life is short and for some of us, shorter than others. I stared again at the pictures of Sydney and Aiden. I prayed for time with them, LOTS and lots of time, with many moments that would take our breath away.

Finishing up a silent double header of Hail Mary and the Lord's Prayer, I complied with an LPN by the name of Sarah who came by to take my temperature and blood pressure. After she was finished, I pushed the arms of my chair forward which brought my legs and feet up. Although it wasn't even 8:30 am and I hadn't begun treatment, I was starting to feel tired. I closed my eyes and saw the tumbling surf of Neskowin roll toward the shore, but before I could feel the frigid water touch my toes, Tracy returned with a forlorn look on her face.

"I'm really sorry to have to tell you this, but the pictures of your port placement show its catheter is in too close proximity of the heart muscle. Dr. Sharman wants us to administer your Gazyva today through a vein in your hand or arm until we can get this matter resolved."

"Shit," I said, not being a strong tea bag at all. "Sorry," followed quickly.

"If I were you, I'd say 'Shit' too," said Tracy. "No reason to apologize, none whatsoever."

"What exactly does Sharman mean about getting the matter resolved?" questioned my husband.

"Well, he's trying right now to talk directly with Dr. Stack. The problem is Dr. Sharman has patients back to back this morning and Salem Hospital said Stack is in surgery for a while longer. If absolutely necessary, and I know this is the last thing you want to hear right now, is you could have your port removed and reinserted again." Tracy took a deep breath and then added, "Or you could have chemo each session through a vein other than a port."

" FUBAR," I stated matter-of-factly. My go to acronym of 'Fucked Up Beyond All Recognition' seemed highly appropriate at this time in my life.

John came over and kissed my forehead before asking, "What do you want to do, Rabbit?"

"Go home and pretend this isn't happening," I sighed. He grinned and Tracy looked worried as I added, "Let's light this candle, do what Sharman said and get things started. But first I need to pee. And I mean REALLY pee."

"You go to the bathroom, Pam, and I'll get your drugs and round up our best infusion nurse to get a line ready." She moved in overdrive while I took baby steps to the head.

Opening the door, the lovely aroma of vanilla covered what had been the antiseptic smell of the treatment room. It was like I'd found an oasis in the midst of a desert of cancer cells. The room was spacious and sparkled in its cleanliness; germs would have a hard time taking a foothold in this place. I did my business and the toilet flushed as I stood. Washing with the available pump soap, I spied the nearby outlet that was home to the vanilla and inhaled deeply before returning to my reserved recliner.

Tracy, Betty, John, Katy the infusion nurse, and a grey-haired lady with a tray of alcohol wipes, thin tubing, and butterfly needles awaited my arrival. It was 9:00 am. I sat in my special chair, and Betty was the first to speak.

"Here are your blood test results. Also, Gazyva is given today, and both it and Bendamustine on Thursday and Friday. Absolutely don't take Allopurinal on Benda days, but you will resume the Allopurinal on Saturday the 15th, the same day you will need your Neulasta."

"How do I get my Neulasta when Salem Oncology where I was going for my shots aren't open on Saturdays?"

"We'll arrange for a Neulasta patch to be administered here on Friday after your treatment and it will automatically deliver the drug on Saturday," said Tracy. "Each month going forward you can decide whether you want the Neulasta in shot or patch form. Your insurance will cover all the $12,000 cost but about $370.00 per dosage."

All I could think of again was, "Thank God, I have a $2500 yearly out of pocket limit insurance plan!"

The tray lady wrapped my left hand and lower arm in a heating pad and readied her supplies. After a minute or so she inserted the needle in a vein between my thumb and forefinger and hooked me up to the pre-meds.

Medicines in liquid form like Methylprednisolone, Dexamethasone and Hydrocortisone were intended to prevent release of substances in my body that might cause inflammation of things like my skin, joints, lungs and other organs. Another drug, Palonosetron, was for nausea and vomiting. It would be really nice if that med could keep my lovely vanilla scented bathroom from turning into a place of hurling stomach debris. Diphenhydramine was added to the mix and as an antihistamine treated symptoms of an allergic reaction and also had the wonderful effect of making patients like me very sleepy.

Finally, I swallowed two Tylenol, each 500 mg, and busy Sarah once more took my temp and blood pressure. I bid a fond farewell to the grey-haired phlebotomist, which to this day I'm sorry to say, still remains nameless. John covered me from chin to toes with a nicely warmed blanket and I took slow, tiny sips from my water bottle and later added apple juice from my bag. Beyond the pictures of my grandchildren, I again stared at the horse that now had moved from the pile of hay to take cover under a giant fir offering shade from the morning sun. For 45 minutes I rested while the pre-meds did their job. Everything was peaceful and wonderfully calm, as it is so many times before a terrible storm.

Katy brought over my bag of Gazyva and hung it in place of my pre-meds. I expected it to be some evil color red, but instead it looked like a bag full of innocent water. Before hooking it up to my line, she checked off a list of things on a form with 'Pam Johnson' at the top of it. Then Gazyva started its trip inside me.

Tracy stood close by and gently touching the back of my right hand said, "Everything will be alright. Keep talking to us once we get started and tell us how you're feeling. Even the smallest sensation, no matter what it is, tell us about it right away. Try to relax, Pam, but listen to what your body is telling you. Okay?"

A soft, "Okay," filtered across my lips. John mustered a tiny smile and the drip, drip continued.

I didn't feel a thing for awhile; I just sat in my chair and tried to pass the time by telling Tracy about our grandkids and the different places I'd taught during my career. John chimed in about our tennis feats and the tournaments we'd won over the years and how we both looked forward to getting back on the courts again as a mixed doubles pair. Eight minutes were completely uneventful, but then suddenly I thought I felt my heart skip a beat, but I wasn't sure. Was it real or imagined? Did I experience what I thought was a skip or thought I felt it because I expected to feel it?

Rather than arouse needless worry among my audience, I decided to say nothing for the time being. My body had felt so many things over the years; "electrical shocks" across my chest from the cutting of nerves during my double mastectomy, tingling along my Merkel scars, dry mouth because of an extracted salivary gland, edema in my right arm because of lymph node removal, eyelid twitching from the stress of teaching teenagers and criminals, and heart skipping for romantic and nonromantic reasons. I was a bundle of human sensations ready to manifest themselves at any given moment so I believed the prudent thing to do was wait, wait a little bit to make absolutely sure I'd felt something concrete. I drank more water and adjusted my bottom in the chair and listened to Tracy share a little about her basketball playing in college and beyond as she continued to check her watch and take my pulse. What do you know; I'd been right about her athletic gait and sport of choice.

A minute later another beat skipped and this time it was paired with some light-headedness. The two were so gentle and fleeting I thought they couldn't be hard and fast side-effects. WRONG! Yes, the full blown effects would be stronger and fiercer, but what I was feeling was the warning shot of the explosion soon to follow. In no time and out of nowhere, my pulse quickened, my heart raced, I was hot, dizzy and nauseous. Turning white as a sheet I blurted out, "I feel SICK!"

Immediately, and I mean STAT, Tracy pushed the recliner as far back as it would go, John put a pillow under my feet and Katy stopped the flow of Gazyva. Sarah brought over a barf bag and then took my blood pressure. A call was put into Sharman and the wait began to see what else my body was going to do. I held on. Tracy took my temperature and tried to help me calm my breathing. "In...out.......in...... out............in.............out," she repeated over and over again. I tried my hardest to be a good patient and follow her advice.

With clammy hands getting clammier and a putrid taste coming up through my throat, I was helpless to stop what came next. After a few dry heaves into the blue accordion looking bag, vomit streamed out of my mouth, accompanied by loud, wrenching noises. My husband, bless his ever loving heart, put the sight, sound, and smell of me aside and tenderly wiped my forehead with a damp cloth.

I closed my eyes tightly to stop the room from spinning and held on for dear life. Time passed. Then, almost as quickly as I went downhill, I started back up. It was like being in the throes of hard labor one moment and then the next moment being out of pain because a contraction ended. My heart slowed its racing, my head no longer felt light, the urge to vomit was replaced with a desire for a plain bagel with cream cheese and I was starting to feel like me again.

"Jesus Christ. What just happened?" I asked no one in particular.

"How do you feel?" questioned a concerned Tracy who was strapping on the blood pressure cup again. "What happened is you had some side-effects; almost exactly at the time other patients experienced theirs. The adverse reactions are fairly common for first time infusions, but that doesn't make them any less frightening. I'm so sorry you had to go through that, Pam. Fortunately, your body handled things pretty well. Your color is already starting to return and that's GREAT!"

"I'm feeling better," I told Tracy, but kept to myself the strange visions I'd seen with closed eyes; they were wonderful and terrible at the same time. I remembered I was inside a giant red balloon floating towards the clouds. Tracy, Katy, Sarah, and John were jumping on trampolines, trying to grab the balloon's long string and yelling at me not to pop it with the needle in my arm because I'd fall and kill myself. My dead father also joined in the jumping and suddenly yelled up at me, 'Pam, being dead doesn't hurt, but dying does.' He said it over and over again. Then somebody yanked on the string, the balloon popped and I crashed into my chair. When I opened my eyes, everyone was around me... except for my dad.

"How do you feel now?" John asked.

"A lot better; really, a lot better.

"Are you sure, Rabbit? questioned my hubby a second time as he gave the Gazyva bag a menacing look.

"Really, I feel MUCH better. Pinky swear."

"But is this going to happen again?" I asked Tracy.

"It shouldn't. Other people in the trial, like I said, had the same side-effects of dizziness, low blood pressure, increased heart rate and vomiting as you at about the same time into the first dosage, but when the infusion was resumed, no adverse symptoms appeared. Not then and not on subsequence treatment days. And with Bendamustine, side-effects very, very rarely occurred. Also, you recovered quickly and that's always a good sign."

Dr. Sharman came up behind me and made his presence known with a calm, "Understand you had a rough few minutes, Pam. How are you doing now?" He took a chair next to mine.

"Everyone is taking good care of me. I'm doing okay, now."

"Good, good," he repeated. "We're going to let you rest a while before we start the Gazyva again. And we're going to give you a little more of the pre-meds first. Things should go much more smoothly from now on out. If you feel like a little something to snack on, do it. And remember to drink plenty of water." He was gone in a flash to attend to his other patients, but not before he left behind a gentle pat on my shoulder.

I relaxed in my recliner and dozed off for a good 20 minutes, thanks to more of the Benadryl and other pre-Gazyva drugs. When I opened my eyes, John was scanning the American Soccer magazine he'd brought from home and Tracy was joining us with some good news.

"Well, Dr. Sharman and Dr. Stack just got off the phone with each other. Your port placement meets all of Salem Hospital's protocols and has been deemed perfectly safe for treatment here. Sharman has given his approval for infusion by way of your Power Port. That means starting tomorrow you'll no longer be poked and prodded in that left arm or hand. "How does that sound?"

"Thank God," I answered as my husband closed his magazine and approval crossed his face. "I needed something good to happen today."

A beeping noise signaled my extra bag of pre-meds was empty and Katy hooked me up to the Gazyva, again. I took a deep breath and nervously commenced the slow infusion of the G. We passed the nine minute mark and then well beyond with no bad side-effects sidelining me. "Halleluiah," I said to myself, "Gazyva really was better the second time around."

Every half hour I walked the 25 yards to the bathroom, still attached to my IV machine which automatically switched to battery power when not plugged into its electrical outlet. Tracy had shown me the ins and outs of maneuvering the room without ramming into people and obstacles, and most importantly, how to lower myself up and down on the toilet without disconnecting any of my lines. This was a time honored skill I needed to master, since staying hydrated always involved frequent trips to the WC.

Finally, it was close to noon and relief settled over me. I felt like any dues I owed must have been paid during that first scary infusion of Gazyva. John relaxed a bit too and his gaze at the Gazyva was now without total disdain.

The next hours came and went slowly, with the infusion rate of Gazyva carefully calculated for my health and safety. The drug was killing thousands and thousands of immortal lymphocytes at an amazing speed even though it was taking hours to empty the small bag. If the Allopurinal was doing its job, and I sure hoped it was, in the days to come the chemicals and salts released by those dead lymphocytes wouldn't cause low blood pressure, kidney damage or tumors. I'd had enough chemo induced side-effects already. Sarah continued checking my pulse rate, oxygen levels, temperature and blood pressure as she'd done ever since I'd arrived in the treatment room early that morning.

By 1:45 pm I was pretty hungry and devoured a Starbuck's Chonga bagel covered in Philadelphia cream cheese and then followed that with a mint chocolate almond protein bar. Both were delicious and the definite highlight of my Wednesday thus far. The following two hours were spent mostly napping, playing solitaire on my iPad and some light reading of People Magazine articles about the sexiest men in Hollywood over 60 and which Kardashian was dating who.

At 5:00 pm my IV machine beeped again, this time signaling my treatment for the day with Gazyva was finished. Katy drew blood from my line for another round of tests so they could be compared with the morning's results. By the time she had my post-meds hooked up and flowing, Tracy marched to my side with an award winning smile on her face. She handed me the sheet that compared my results from early morning to 5:20pm. The two reflected astounding differences!

My WBC count had gone from a high of 131.6 critical value testing, down to 20.3 high, and my lymphocytes had decreased from 98.95 to 18.58. Dr. Sharman had told me the cancer cells would die quickly, but this was almost unbelievable. No wonder that Allopurinal was so darn important.

Of course some things lowered that I didn't want to go down, like my RBC count from 3.83 to 3.14. These are the red blood cells that carry oxygen throughout my entire body and are VERY important. HGB had decreased to 9.7 from 11.9, indicating a significant change in hemoglobin, a protein produced by my bone marrow that's stored in my red blood cells. Hemoglobin helps red blood cells to transport oxygen from my lungs to my body through my arteries. It also transports $CO2$ (carbon dioxide) from around my body back to my lungs through my veins. Simply put, hemoglobin is what makes red blood cells red. Platelets, red blood cells that help control bleeding moved from 134 to just 54 and my all-important infection fighting Neutrophils dipped to 1.06

from 6.05. Tracy assured me all my results were great and as the trial continued, the goal of combining Bendamustine and Gazyva (BG) was to further lower my WBC and Lymphocyte counts and raise back up to normal the other blood components. The patients who had come before me had proven this the case and now we Phase II participants would hopefully prove it more convincingly.

The post-meds took about an hour, so it was quickly approaching 6:30 pm. Tracy had taken over Sarah's job of routine monitoring my vitals and Katy removed the IV from my hand and bandaged up the bruised area where the needle had penetrated. We were the only people left in the treatment room.

"Hope you get overtime pay," I joked.

"We always stay as long as our patients, no matter what time it is," Tracy replied. "You can't get rid of us," Katy laughed.

"Have a safe drive back to Keizer," added Tracy. "We'll see you bright and early tomorrow morning. And remember, no Allopurinal for the next two days because you'll be getting Bendamustine." She paused and then concluded with, "You did real good today, both of you."

We gathered up our things, and I carefully placed Syd and Aiden's pictures back in my purse for safe-keeping. My two grandkids had kept close watch over me and I believe with my whole heart that they and my dad were the ones who pulled on that string and brought me back down to earth.

John got me home safely around 8:00 pm. Although pretty exhausted, I settled sweet Charlie on my lap and then together the three of us watched CNN. Anderson Cooper and Don Lemmon reported that the world, although full of problems, was being pretty well taken care of by President Obama and Vice-President Biden. I agreed.

It felt like we'd been gone for a whole lot longer than just a day. While John called Karin to check in and put a positive spin on my first encounter with chemotherapy, I drank more Smart Water from the bottle that my husband always planted close-by. Charlie lifted his chin high and purred contently as I scratched the spot of white fur under his jaw.

"How are the kids doing?" I asked Johnny when he joined me on the couch.

"Everyone's fine. They want to come over tomorrow after dinner to see you. Syd and Aiden have made cards and Karin and Drew have flowers. I told them tomorrow would be good. Hope that was alright."

"Tomorrow," I repeated. "I sure need some kiddo time. Want them to know Grandma's chemo is doing a good job of killing her cancer cells. Telling them 'Yes,' was more than alright."

We switched the channel to less serious faire and chose a re-run of THE BIG BANG THEORY. The antics of a group of VERY smart, but socially awkward scientists and their relationships with others never failed to make us laugh.

The particular episode we watched had to do with the absurdity of their roommate agreement between the two leading characters, experimental physicist Leonard Hofstadter and theoretical physicist Sheldon Cooper. They argued because Leonard brought home a girlfriend and they had sex in his bedroom, but the next morning Sheldon was beside himself because he hadn't been given the 12 hour warning about intercourse. They had a silly roommate agreement and I had a serious Consent Form, both vowed to by those involved. It was a classic BIG BANG and for half an hour I laughed and shoved chemo way, way, to the back of my mind.

By the time the credits rolled across the screen I was in a wonderful state, relishing every second of my temporary nirvana. I nodded off and stopped stroking Charlie's fur. He politely meowed his displeasure before jumping down and heading to the garage where John had put a small can of Friskies Buffet in his food bowl. My hubby and I climbed the stairs together, him leading the way with my hand in his. We hugged gently and kissed before parting into our own bedrooms. "Love you, Rabbit," he called out from behind his closed door. "Love you too, Squirrel," I answered from behind mine.

Stripping naked, I stood in front of the portable air-conditioner lodged in the window. Its breeze cooled my hot flesh and with my finger tips, I delicately tapped the skin covering my port. It would be my companion for the next six months and maybe longer.

My CLL Buddy, Brett Hall, still had his in after finishing treatment months ago. Betty had told me some people just liked having their ports around, close at hand like a good luck charm or a BFF. Right now I viewed my port as a novel companion designed to make life easier, to assist me in my part time job before I returned to full time living. It hadn't traveled into the 'friend's zone,' yet.

That night I dreamed, not about a red balloon, but about riding on the back of a huge dragon with GAME of THRONES' Daenerys Storm-born Targaryen. My hands were wrapped around her tiny waist as we flew high in the sky and circled the lands below. Our travels were magical; I was unafraid and wanted nothing more than to go faster, and faster, and faster. We were women warriors who'd defeated the Seven Kingdoms' strongest men in battle and were celebrating the final victory of a final war. As our ride came to an end, our dragon slowly swooped down, skirting the tree tops before landing in front of our beloved people. We offered them our blessings and everyone cheered. Suddenly, my alarm blasted 5:30 am and like so many dreams, its pleasures were cut short. The second day of treatment was here.

We arrived at WVCI early to the greetings of Tracy and Katy's twin Jordan, also a treatment nurse. The sisters were definite doppelgangers and even their voices were the same in sound and cadence. My place of prominence, the "Reserved" recliner, was in use by another patient so I was guided two chairs away, giving the newbie extra room and privacy should she run into problems like I did yesterday. My temperature was taken with a thermometer under my tongue, and the pulse oximeter on my finger measured the amount of oxygen saturation in my blood. Both were normal.

Jordan came over and checked the placement of my port in the left side of my chest, cleaned the skin around it and then asked if I wanted some cold numbing spray before she inserted the IV for pre-meds.

"Might as well give it a try. Anything that numbs the spot where a needle is going in sounds like a good idea to me," I voiced my approval and she sprayed away.

John settled in a chair by mine and again placed Sydney and Aiden's pictures on the windowsill. Their photos were next to a saying written in erasable yellow marker, "I have cancer; cancer doesn't have me." Also on the windowpane and this one given credit to Mary Anne Radmacher, stated, "Courage doesn't always roar. Sometimes courage is the little voice at the end of the day that says I'll try again tomorrow." It was my tomorrow yesterday; the second day of the BG clinical trial.

Jordan instructed me to take a deep breath and hold it for a second while she quickly inserted the IV needle. It was a cinch compared to searching for a vein in my hand or arm and hoping to find one good enough for a long day's journey into chemo therapy. She taped the hanging needle and tubing with a clear piece of adhesive resembling Saran Wrap so everything would stay put. Then she quickly started my premeds just like yesterday. Tracy explained the plan; Gazyva would be administered first, slowly, followed by Bendamustine at a quicker rate. She told me it was **highly** unlikely that I'd experience any bad side-effects. I knew there were no absolute guarantees, but felt confident she was right.

"How'd you sleep last night?" she asked me.

I replied with, "Not exactly like a baby, but I sure had a good dream."

"Really? What was it?" quizzed my husband.

"Well, let's just say I was on the back of Drogon with Emilia Clarke." John grinned knowingly while Tracy was completely lost about the TV series, GOT and my breath-taking ride with a lovely Targaryen. Tracy didn't ask for further explanation of my dream and quickly moved on to more pressing issues at hand.

"Remember Pam, if you need anything to help you sleep, let me know. Getting enough rest is important during your treatment. Also, if you want a prescription of lidocaine cream to take away the discomfort of that needle being stuck in your port, just say the word. All you'd have to do is apply the cream one hour before you get here and cover it with a Press 'N Seal to keep it off your clothes.

"Thanks. Think I'm alright for now. I'm sleeping okay and that cold spray pretty much did the trick. If I have a problem down the line I'll sure say something about it."

The sun shined through the treatment windows, making the colorful messages come even more alive. The tiny clouds outside were whisper thin and floating eastward, backed by a beautiful shade of blue. The old horse stood still in her pasture while the woman in the "Reserved" recliner threw up all over the floor and Betty rushed over to help. I studied the first timer with pity and then remembered myself in the same location just one day ago, struggling with all my might to come back from my own wild ride of awful side-effects.

The pre-meds flowed, and I took my Tylenol right on schedule. When I made my trip to the bathroom it was a little trickier because this time the IV was dangling from my chest and not taped in place at my wrist where it'd felt more secure. With my over active imagination, it wasn't hard to picture the darn thing falling out from the sheer force of gravity and expensive drugs suddenly spewing out over the linoleum. So, to prevent such a catastrophe I used extra tiny baby steps and tip-toed extra slowly to the toilet, but only first after unplugging my machine from the wall socket and trusting battery power to travel the familiar pathway.

I avoided getting too close to the poor woman who'd just thrown up; some semblance of privacy in such a non-private atmosphere was the least I could do for her. Once back to my wall socket I searched my cell phone and had John take a picture of me to send to Karin, accompanied by a short motherly text. I posed with a tilted smile courtesy of my facial Merkel surgery and raised my right hand in a sign of peace. John captured my image well and I attached it to a text that read, "Everything going fine. Looking forward to seeing the Monekes tonight! Love ya, Mama ☺"

After eating an orange, Caesar salad, and playing Sudoku on my iPad, it was time for the Gazyva. Jordan stopped the pre-meds and Tracy returned from making phone calls in her office and we all keyed up for the second time event. I watched the drug drip, drip, drip into my port and on into my veins while the minutes snailed by. Then more and more minutes and nothing happened, absolutely nothing. I felt fine, no light-headedness, no vomiting, no racing heartbeat, no hot flash, no side-effects whatsoever. NOTHING was a good thing, a wonderful thing!

My phone made its usual melodic response to an incoming message, and I found out Karin had gotten my picture and text and shared both with Drew, Syd, and Aiden. Everyone sent their love and were excited to see me that night, but first I had to finish here and asked Tracy when that might be.

"Because you're doing so good, Dr. Sharman said we could speed up the Gazyva a little bit and Bendamustine can always be given pretty quickly. Then we need to follow that with your post-meds and flushing of your port. If all goes well, I'd say you could be out of here by 4:00 pm. How does that sound?"

"A lot better than 7:00 pm last night," I responded.

My spirits lifted even higher as I again stared at the pictures of Syd and Aiden, remembering them as tiny babies cradled in my arms and then like yesterday taking their first wobbly steps. How cute they were when we played 'peek-a-boo' and hide and seek, and how they loved bedtime stories like GOODNIGHT MOON, GREEN EGGS and HAM, IF YOU GIVE a MOUSE a COOKIE, CORDUROY and so many more. I'd yearned for them to get out of diapers and be potty trained, and now I missed seeing their tiny bum bums and smelling Pampers. I wanted them to master feeding themselves, and now I longed for a return to the days when I played airplane to get them to open their mouths to rice cereal and Gerber's strained carrots. I'm probably no different than any other grandmother, but darn it, time goes by too fast when our children are young, and then it races to the finish line when we have grandchildren.

The treatment went by much better than it did the day before. No adverse side-effects really lifted my spirits and the pictures of two little children helped me believe in a future of remission from CLL, forever long I had no idea. Even with only a single day's experience of chemo, I felt a little like a veteran already. Maybe it was because I'd gone through so much shit yesterday, that I thought there wasn't a whole lot more left to happen. Silly, silly me.

Minutes, and then hours went by without incident. It was amazing how NOT having trouble finding a vein and poking a needle in it could brighten my day. All the drugs pouring into my body went in without any problems and my temp, blood pressure and oxygen levels were 'A' okay all day long. I could have sworn the blankets were warmer, my Smart water was colder and the bathroom more lemony. Everything was wonderful, except for one annoying problem that'd really started to bug me. The area under the tape on my chest was red, irritated and itched nonstop. It wasn't poison ivy or mosquito itchy, but bothersome enough I wanted to get it off and never use it again.

Hearing the last beep on the IV machine meant my treatment was done and all that needed doing was the flushing of my port. Jordan came over, as well as Tracy, to finish off day 2 of a total of 15 by the end of December. Saline solution was injected into my port and flowed down the catheter to prevent clogging and the chance of blood clots forming. Then the IV needle was pulled painlessly from my chest and the bothersome tape removed to uncover what I was feeling. It was a unanimous decision that I'd be switching to PAPER strips tomorrow; problem solved. Finally, Jordan applied a small band aid over my port area, and I moved one step closer to getting out the door.

"You're doing great," remarked Tracy, "Hear you get to see those grandkids tonight."

"Ya," I said, "Should see them in a few hours. Know they're really worried about me."

I got up from the chair and carefully picked up my special photos. I looked at Tracy and continued, "We told Sydney I have cancer and am taking special medicine to help it go away, keeping things as simple as we could. She understands a lot more than Aiden who only really knows that Grandma has a big spleen and needs to be careful so it doesn't get hurt when we play."

"How old are they again?"

"Syd's eight and Aiden's five," cut in John who had already gathered up my belongings and was pushing his chair back to the empty treatment station nearby.

"Such fun ages," Tracy said. "I sure remember my kids at that time in their lives."

Then she continued with, "Tomorrow is your last treatment for the week and you'll have four days off before another one. Only Benda tomorrow too so that's good. And remember, because your infection preventing Neulasta must be administered 24 hours after tomorrow's treatment and that's a Saturday, we'll arrange for a patch instead. It'll allow you to take the medicine at home. We'll explain how the patch works and then put it on your arm and you or John can just take it off once the medicine's been injected into your system. Lots of our patients like doing it that way instead of a shot in a doctor's office." She looked at me strangely and asked, "Did I already tell you all this?"

"I don't remember," I lied. "I'm at the age where hearing things more than once is a necessity and never a bother."

"Please, be sure to let me know if you need additional anti-nausea medication. Some patients try a variety of them before they find the one that works best, or a combination of pills that finally help. Most patients who are farther along in the trial than you are didn't experience bad nausea until about the 3rd day after they were home. We don't want you feeling so bad you stop eating and believe me, there's nothing like the urge to throw up to keep a person from breakfast, lunch and dinner. My goal is for you NOT to lose weight these next six months. So, let's stay on top of this nausea thing, agreed?"

"Agreed," I came back strongly. I'd learned all too well during my first treatment that I couldn't simply power through the chemo's side-effects. I'm no mixed martial arts expert like Ronda Rousy, but I'm no shrinking violet either. Chemo side effects sidelined me and can sideline anyone...body strength and mental toughness can't win over drugs that always have the upper hand over even the most courageous of cancer fighters.

Tracy smiled as I finished with, "I pretty much learned my lesson about trying to second guess myself about these drugs and how they can bring me down. And with a weekend approaching, I think I better take you up on your offer."

"Glad to hear you say that. I'll have some prescriptions ready for you tomorrow."

"Thanks, Tracy."

"No problem."

On the way out I went into my pretty vanilla scented bathroom and was repulsed by what I found. The toilet seat was up, yellow drops of urine centered the inside of the lid and blotted the seat, a scrunched up paper towel hadn't made it to the garbage can, and the place smelled like its previous resident had passed a bucket full of gas. I controlled the urge to hunt the culprit down and give him a piece of my mind and instead cut the male visitor some slack for the errors of his way. All of us at this place, whether patient or non-patient, were going through hard times coping with the Big C and all the forms it came in. Everybody definitely had more pressing things on their minds than leaving a bathroom as they found it. I left the scene and relieved myself in the toilet at the other end of the treatment room; it smelled of lavender, not a favorite of mine.

With chemo finished for the day, John and I got in the car and left Springfield behind us. I relaxed in the seat beside him and keyed in on my surroundings as we headed north. Sheep, lots of them, dotted the fields on either side of the Interstate; all of them eating to their hearts' content and oblivious to the possibility of one day ending up a seasoned lamb chop at Applebee's. If their future truly was slaughter and not the selling of wool, at least they were experiencing the good life for a while.

Cows and horses replaced sheep in the fields before long, and then wheat in Marion County replaced the ryegrass of rural Linn. Farmers in the cabs of their air-conditioned John Deere tractors plowed fields whose crops had already been harvested, leaving huge plumes of dust in their wake, and watching them my mind hop-scotched to the past.

When I was a little girl, one of my all time best things to do was go with my sisters and mom to pick up my dad from work at A. C. Hague's Farm Equipment and Supply. It was located across from the fair grounds, a place bustling with farmers, especially during the months of August and September. Inside the display room was the cutest miniature Deere tractor any kid could ever hope to peddle. It was painted forest green with the name brand in bright yellow and the seat was real leather, sleek and soft.

We three kids got to ride the little Deere once every time we picked up our daddy, but that didn't stop us from begging Mr. Hague for second turns. Unfortunately, he was steadfast in keeping the three-wheeler in pristine condition, unspoiled by the pleas of Mel's children. I drove Silverton Road a while back and went by the place dad used to work. Today the A. C. Hague building is inhabited by Pronto Signs and resides on a much busier Silverton Road then it was in the 1950's. Although my chances of ever riding a Deere again are pretty weak, maybe I'll add it to my Bucket List and make it happen one day. After all, a repeat of a childhood joy is always a possibility and being a grandma is absolute proof of that.

Taking the Keizer exit brought me back to the here and now. "What time are the kids coming over?" I asked John again.

"Pretty sure they said around 7:00 pm. Are you hungry? Want me to stop somewhere and get you something to eat?"

Without hesitation I replied an enthusiastic, Kentucky Fried Chicken!

"You got it, Rabbit," my husband said, his tired face no longer looking so tired.

We drove to the colonel's and I ordered an original chicken dinner with mashed potatoes and gravy and biscuit with butter and honey. John, not being a fan of the red state menu, decided on two beef burritos at Taco Bell.

We devoured our meals on TV tables, classic Johnson style, while viewing a few minutes of CNN before switching to 'on demand' reruns of old SNL clips. We were in stitches as always watching Justin Timberlake and Andy Samberg's 'D*ck in a Box', which by the way, for us rates right up there with Alex Baldwin's routine of 'Schweddy Balls' and Chris Farley's 'Chippendale Audition' with Patrick Swayze.

Team Moneke opened the front door and announced their arrival with, "Anyone home?" We answered with, "We sure are. Come on in." Then Squirrel hastily pushed down on the remote's power button and blackened our TV screen before under-aged grandchildren had the opportunity to see boxes covering peoples' private parts.

Two little kids slowly approached us with guarded smiles and homemade cards in their hands, while their mother and father looked relieved by the grins on our faces and warm welcome. Karin placed a beautiful bouquet of gerbera daisies and baby's breath on my old hutch within easy viewing and Drew handed me my favorite iced coffee from Starbuck's. "It's so good to see you guys," I managed to get out before tears welled.

"What's wrong, Grandma?" Sydney asked immediately, serious concern in her little girl voice.

"I'm just so happy to see you guys. Nothing's wrong...I'm just so happy to see all of you." I used a Kleenex from my pocket and then continued with, "And thanks for the flowers and Starbuck's. You know exactly what I like."

"The kids made you some cards, Mom," said Karin. "Want to see them?"

"There's nothing I'd like better." And with that two little human beings settled on either side of me on the couch, slowly and with great care. It was apparent that Grandma's port had been another topic of conversation before leaving their home, just like an enlarged spleen had been a while back.

Aiden's card had a picture of a very large, black dog with an orange cat on its back and inside he'd phonetically spelled, "I luv yu." And the card from Syd was decorated with a picture of the beach with seagulls flying in the sky over the ocean waves and below she'd written, "Grandma, I love you to the moon and the sun and the stars and Neskowin and back." I shared the cards with John and then with their little eyes watching my every move, I carefully displayed them on our refrigerator, a place of honor where they knew I'd look at them every day.

Team Monekes' visit was brought to a halt when I couldn't stop my first yawn at 7:30 pm and though I pleaded for them to stay longer, was voted down five to one. Thankfully, their brief stay was enough to reassure everyone, especially the grandkids, that I was doing okay and that Grandpa was taking extra good care of me. We hugged our good-byes.

"You remember when Syd asked us if people were dead longer than they were alive?" I questioned my husband as we again viewed their cards together.

"Sure do. And do you remember when she didn't want to take a nap at our house and lodged her complaint by telling us that when she was asleep she didn't feel like she was here so she wanted to stay awake?"

"Boy do I!" I exclaimed. "Do you think Aiden will be like her when he gets a little older? You know, a deep thinker, kind of an old soul in a young body?" I asked.

"Yep, no doubt about it," my husband chuckled. "Wouldn't have it any other way."

"Me either," I said, as another yawn escaped.

By 8:00 pm, Charlie was in the garage and I was in bed sipping iced coffee and thinking more and more about Sydney and Aiden. Those little human beings, those blonde-haired balls of joy and energy were the main reason I decided to take on a clinical trial. I was just getting to know them and they, me. Our relationship had only really started and I craved more time with them; the thought of not having years and years devastated me beyond measure.

Even though I was sleepy, I couldn't drift off. My mind raced thinking about the 13 chemo sessions I had left and then dwelled on the many adjustments I'd made because of cancers present and past. Some of these alterations were minor and temporary, like avoiding my left side where a delicate spleen bulged and a port was homed. Another change though was major and permanent; this was the loss of my breasts.

Not wanting reconstructive surgery but wanting to look like my boobs hadn't gone anywhere, my life- long change meant wearing a Soft T or some kind of prosthesis, no matter how awkward both were and uncomfortable they felt. Hoping against the hot flashes of menopause, I even once tried a pair of adhesive, skin colored falsies, but their considerable weight couldn't put up with the heat I generated. Unfortunately, it was during 4th period College Writing at South Salem High School that, on their maiden voyage, both boobies unattached themselves and traveled all the way down to my waistline. It certainly was a disturbing sight for young people to take in and me to experience, but I made the best of a bad situation and gleefully commented, "Well,

Mr. Newton was sure right about his gravity!" We all got a good laugh before I excused myself to the faculty bathroom across the hall and pulled off my false attachments. Not much later I removed all pretenses of carrying around that which wasn't mine and decided to forever go without fake knockers.

On Thursday, August 13th, 2015, John and I again started our trip toward Willamette Valley Cancer Institute and Research Center. Traffic was light and the temperature, an already warm 75 degrees. Bendamustine would soon flow through my veins and because the occurrence of tumor lysis syndrome occurred in fewer than 1% of Benda patients, Allopurinal was one less drug needed in my system that day. Gazyva, well that was a different story.

This time as we traveled the interstate things heightened in clarity and my veiled existence became raw with discovery. Sights, smells, sounds, taste and touch, those things that signal the world around us moved from behind a curtain to take center stage. Perhaps fighting for one's life naturally brings the world closer to us, makes us truly see things we didn't see before, turning neglect into intimacy.

I noticed for the first time a Carl's Junior sign that told me it was the 'Pioneer of the Great American Burger'; spotted the words, 'Calapooia' at milestone 30 in recognition of one of many local Native American tribes; learned from a faded billboard that Linn County was actually the 'Grass Seed Capital of the World' and I pondered why every barn spotted next to a farmhouse was painted red.

The stench from Albany's old paper mill hit me harder than ever before and the diesel smell from the semi-truck in front of us diminished the beauty of the landscape. When John popped orange Tic Tac's in his mouth I felt like a fruity perfume had come to my rescue.

Lady Gaga belted the words from 'Born This Way' and instead of only hearing the melody, I listened intently to the lyrics. She was bearing her soul; telling the world there's nothing wrong with being who you REALLY are.

My mama told me when I was young
We are all born superstars
She rolled my hair and put my lipstick on
in the glass of her boudoir

"There's nothing wrong with loving who you are"
She said: "Cause He made you perfect, babe
So hold your head up girl, and you'll go far
Listen to me when I say"

I'm beautiful in my way
Cause God makes no mistakes
I'm on the right track, baby
I was born this way

Don't hide yourself in regret
Just love yourself, and you're set
I'm on the right track, baby
I was born this way.

As we approached the exit to Corvallis, home of Oregon State and Aiden's beloved Beaver football team, all my heightened awareness of sight, smell and sound, suddenly turned to feelings of fear. I'd been worried for quite some time because our 'little man' had added football to his list of favorite team sports. The thought of him moving beyond flag football with his best bud, Caleb, and putting on a Riddell helmet to crash heads with other players tore me apart.

I used to like football; in fact, it's fair to say I LOVED football; it was the epitome of amazing strength, strategy, and skill. While a cheerleader at McNary High School, I couldn't wait to watch my boyfriend, Neil Bryant, catch a spiral on Friday nights and carry the pigskin down the sideline in his tight, sexy uniform to the roar of adoring fans. I never gave any thought to him getting his head banged so badly inside his helmet that his brains sloshed around inside his skull. As a species our anatomy wasn't intended to encounter such force; we're simply not made to withstand the trauma and walk away unscathed. We're not woodpeckers or rams!

Little kids like my grandson are at real risk when they play tackle football, not just high school players, college and professional athletes. I wonder how many Oregon State Beavers, University of Oregon Ducks, Willamette Wildcats, Western Oregon Wolves, and the list goes on and on just here in Oregon, have had concussions that first started happening in grade school. Chronic Traumatic Encephalopathy (CTE) is REAL and even if it doesn't kill football athletes, at the least it has the potential to cause terrible periods of aggression, dementia and mood swings.

I don't see myself as an over-protective grandmother who wants to sissify her grandson. I put my money on the research, the facts that scientists have proven and validated, and believe all nay-sayers should watch the movie, 'Concussion' and listen carefully to Dr. Bennet Omalu. If someone decides their loved ones' heads are safe inside a football helmet, well then at least they've been forewarned and can't shift the blame to others.

As an adult I signed a consent form for the BG clinical trial which listed all the risks, including some pretty gruesome ones. Young football players, regardless of their level, deserve to consent to ALL their risks too. Aiden, his parents and all his grandparents are 100% in favor of him keeping his brain healthy, and saying, "No," to tackle football.

My improved awareness continued and soon we reached the bridge over the McKenzie River. Its brilliant turquoise waters churned westward, forcing tiny white caps to somersault over one another. When I looked back at the river, its water glistened in the morning sunshine. It never looked so beautiful as the OSU exit grew farther and farther behind.

We made the turn onto Martin Luther King Avenue and rounded the curve past the old horse who stood, as Walt Whitman writes in 'Song of Myself, 32', "so placid and self-contained." She chomped her hay and then sneezed out a big piece of snot, never giving notice to my stares. My existence was of no importance to her, but my yearning to know her better was growing stronger.

Once in the treatment room I pulled out my small, high-powered Vanguard binoculars and with great care, adjusted both lenses. Scanning the pasture for my horse, I finally spied her off in the corner. For the first time, I saw long beautiful lashes surrounding her dark brown eyes and little tufts of hair crowding the opening of her ears. As she pulled dandelions from the ground, her yellowed teeth chewed hard and her nostrils flared whenever a new scent arrived. Watching the horse up close and personal made her more than just a four-legged creature who happened to inhabit a tiny barn and two acre fenced in field. She'd moved from being an acquaintance to closer to becoming a friend. Putting away my binoculars and after a good poke in my port, Tracy came to my side as the drugs began their journey. John helped me tuck a wonderfully warm blanket around my cold body and I relaxed. First the pre-meds and then the Benda.

"How ya doing?" questioned Tracy.

"Fine," I answered. "Looking forward to my days at home. Not that I won't miss you guys," I quickly added.

"I really appreciate all the things everyone is doing for me, but it'll be nice just being me for awhile instead of the Pam who's going through chemotherapy."

"No worries," said Tracy. "I completely get it." Then she went on to tell me and John that before treatment ended that day she'd show me about the Neulasta patch and how it injected the infection fighting drug pegfilgrastim into my system. The patch would stimulate growth of new, healthy white blood cells in my body without me ever leaving the comfort of my own home. Sure sounded like a great idea.

"I'll bring the patch to you in a little while and go over the directions," stated Tracy. "With what you know about it already, it should be easy. It pretty much takes care of itself." I downed Smart Water, watched my horse some more, played five card pinochle with my honey and when my blanket lost its warmth, snuggled into a warm one. With only Benda on the menu, the day worked its way to an end a little past noon.

Again I could tell by her footsteps that Tracy was approaching. The timing was perfect; my port had been flushed by the ever efficient Katy and I'd just finished going to the bathroom in a WC free of urine on the seat and a pleasant aroma full of vanilla. I felt lucky and ready for this new experience, 'Neulasta by patch.' Tracy welcomed John to pull up his chair next to us girls and soon she began her explanation of how the small on-body injector worked its magic.

The patch was only a couple inches in length and even less so in width. Tracy told me how to monitor it, being aware of any beeps or lights flashing green or red. Green, goooooood; red, baaaaaad. She then went into the possible side-effects, with one very, very commonly experienced by most of her clinical trial patients; aching in their arms and legs. She advised taking Claritin and either Tylenol or Ibuprofen that night, to get a head start on possible pain and if those over the counter things didn't help, she gave me a number to call for a stronger prescription medication.

Other possible side-effects were less common and downright rare: spleen rupture, lung problems such as acute respiratory distress, allergic reactions of rash, shortness of breath, wheezing, dizziness, swelling around my mouth and eyes, fast heart rate and sweating, sickle cell crises, kidney injury and increased white blood cell count (leukocytosis). "Jesus," I told myself. "This is one powerful drug in such an innocent looking delivery system!"

Tracy then gently placed the patch on the outside of my upper left arm and pressed the adhesive surrounding it onto my skin. The status light flashed green; so far so good.

"After about 27 hours your injector will beep to let you know your dose delivery will begin in two minutes. For almost an hour afterwards check the patch for any bad leaks and if everything looks okay, a beep will sound when the dose delivery is done. A tiny bit of leakage is okay, but a lot around the adhesive site is serious, so call the number I gave you right away if this happens."

When she saw our tense looks, she reassured us with, "Not a single one of our patients have encountered significant leakage with Neulasta patches."

"Glad to hear it," I said while John came in second with, "Me too."

I hardly felt the small companion attached to me, but knew I'd be checking her more than often for the next day until she emptied her contents and I peeled her off. Once she'd done her duty, I'd place her inside the plastic container labeled 'Medical Waste,' which only cost $5.00 courtesy of the WVCI pharmacy, the lowest bill yet charged to my account.

The drive home was uneventful, not counting the three times I checked my patch and read the directions that came with it, four times. The nice green light flashed slowly, about every 10 seconds, and its color was so much nicer than red.

We pulled into our driveway by early afternoon and I took a two hour nap on my bed in the same clothes I'd worn for treatment. I was exhausted in both body and spirit, and too tired to fight the urge to stay awake. My sleep was wonderful, that of a quiet mind free of the torment of crazy dreams or frightful glimpses into life's abyss. Awakened by the sound of dueling lawnmowers, I got up with oily, matted hair and an old face lined by a crumpled, feather pillow.

My capris hung with room to spare across my generous hips and thighs, and the sleeves of my shirt ceased hugging my upper arms. The bulge below my waistline had also begun to fade away. My shedding of pounds wasn't a conscious choice and I'd been advised NOT to lose any while on my 6 month job assignment. I tried for three square meals a day, but treatment was sucking the pleasure out of consumption. Part of me was happy losing weight, but chemotherapy was definitely the wrong way to go about doing it.

Finishing up in the bathroom, I put my Allopurinol on the nightstand as an added reminder to take it tomorrow, and continue that ritual the next 10 days I wasn't on Bendamustine. By my calculations, I'd be swallowing that pill on Saturday just about the time a minuscule needle would poke my arm, helping me again to lower my risk of infection.

The next morning started out perfect. No trip to WVCI for treatment, no nausea yet from the BG, no rain clouds in the sky and a long walk at Minto Brown Park where dogs, unleashed by their owners, ran to their hearts' content. Golden Retrievers, Labradoodles, Collies and mixed breeds great and small; I loved them all, and petting them was a love affair in action!

John and I strolled the paths slowly, holding hands like we often did. The air was pure Oregon, fresh and clean, and the walk was quiet except for happy barking and an occasional call of the wild. Minto did more to make me feel better than anything had for a long, long time. Back in the car I washed my hands with alcohol sanitary wipes, rolled down the window to enjoy the summer breeze and glanced at the dashboard clock...the patch would do its duty in a few hours.

Going home I suddenly felt like I'd just run a marathon with a 20 pound weight on my back and really hit the wall when John pulled into our driveway. I bypassed the lounger in the TV room and headed straight for the nine stairs that'd get me to my Tempur-Pedic. Stretching out on its softness, I mused how not long ago I was introducing myself to some furry friends and then the day took a turn and 'BAM!' I was sprawled out exhausted and ready for sleep and it wasn't even noon.

I gave in to desire for shut eye after downing my Allopurinol and woke up just in time for the beep of the Neulasta patch. I didn't feel even the slightest poke as it started its injection of the costly drug. For the next 45 minutes I checked for leakage and to my great relief, found none. Another beep finally sounded when the dose delivery was complete. Things worked exactly as they were supposed to, but I decided to choose shots for the rest of my Neulasta needs. It wasn't that the patch was inconvenient in any way; it was the chance for error that was unsettling. The red light flashing **could** indicate a serious problem with the device, or the beeping **could** malfunction, or leakage **might** saturate the adhesive and prevent me from getting the full dosage. Way too many variables for this clinical trial enrollee. Even though I'd have to drive 15 minutes to Salem Hematology and wait for the shot, it was worth it. No lights flashing, no beeping; just a good old fashioned poke in the arm.

Even after my nap I still felt tired, just not myself, sort of deflated and without much "umph." Harnessing the Pam in me once again, I pulled a few weeds, watered my veggies and did a small load of laundry.

Watching the world news on TV, especially our country's political scene, brought about uncontrollable eyelid twitching. I watched FOX, CNN and MSNBC to explore a wide range of ideas on many different topics. I'd always taught my students to analyze important issues from various points of view; to "walk in someone else's shoes" and see things as others saw them. Then and only then could a strong argument in defense of one's own opinions take root in the minds of those whose opinions were the opposite. Dueling channels offered opportunities for changing shoes, but also served up lots of stress.

Switching to HGTV, my body reversed back to normal and I smiled watching the Property Brothers reveal a healthy dose of sibling rivalry as Drew found a house for some newlyweds and Jonathan started their remodel with his favorite construction task, demolition day. I watched the twins for half an hour and then returned to my bedroom.

Staying true to form, I checked my bottles of anti-nausea medication again, making sure I had lots of pills on hand. Both Prochlorper, 10mg (also known as Prochlorperazine), and Lorazepam, 1mg, were at attention and ready to go when the urge to vomit presented itself. Tracy had forewarned me that most BG clinical trial patients felt nauseous and puked a few days after treatment, so I figured it'd be Monday or Tuesday, August 17th or 18th, that I'd most likely be in trouble. Hopefully, my stash of pills would keep hurling at a minimum.

The rest of the day was kind of a blur, although I did remember a short walk with my hubby, a spirited game of Monopoly with the grandkids and having very little appetite for much of anything.

Nothing really tasted any good, not even my 'go to take out when sick meal' of pork fried rice from the nearby Chinese restaurant. Trying to down the fortune cookie that came with the order was even harder. Maybe what really got me were the words typed on the tiny piece of paper, "A new challenge is in your future." Geeze, who wrote that shit! I'd had enough new challenges to last a lifetime. I yearned for a cookie whose fortune said, "All will turn out okay as you battle leukemia." Now that was a fortune worth believing in.

Taking Allopurinal Saturday went fine, and my nausea was handled pretty well with medication; only a couple times did I race to the toilet for a lesson in dry heaving. But acid reflux came out of nowhere on Sunday and quickly turned serious. With almost no appetite anyway, now the little pleasure I got from eating only brought on burning pain in my chest that worsened terribly whenever I lay down. My throat hurt badly; I burped, belched, and hic cupped a lot, and the bloating and discomfort in my upper abdomen really worried me. I NEVER expected something called 'acid reflux' to make me feel so awful.

By Monday morning I'd read up on what was happening to my body and knew what products to avoid (chocolate, caffeine, citrus fruits/ juices, fatty/fried foods, tomatoes and tomato products, cheese, mint, garlic, onions and high fat dairy products), and what were good for me (brown rice, oatmeal, herbal tea, carrots, broccoli, green beans, sweet potatoes, bananas, lettuce, celery and melons). That evening I felt better, got a decent night's sleep and the next morning saw no need to worry Tracy with something, which by all appearances, was improving.

Then along came Tuesday, the last day of my home "vacation." And what a day it was. Around 9:00 am I ate a cup of rice and broccoli, with a side of plain wheat toast. All went down without incident and I thought I was in the clear; however, it wasn't acid reflux that got me; it was a giant wave of nausea. A powerful hot flash started things and a yucky taste deep down in my throat moved to its exit. I barely had time to sprint to the toilet before I spewed the escaping goo into my American Standard. I'm not a dainty thrower-upper; those who've heard me say I sound like I'm in the final throes of childbirth, and I've no reason to discount their hearing. When I wretch, I don't give a rat's ass what decibel I hit; all I want is for the agony to stop.

I cleaned my ugly drool and crawled back in bed just in time to do the whole damn thing over and over again. John helped as much as he could with water and sips of 7-up and pills that were supposed to bring an end to my pitiful situation. When things finally settled down late in the afternoon, I weighed myself and compared it to two days ago; I was five pounds lighter. My first day of chemo was looking more and more like child's play.

Chemotherapy and its side-effects are weight-loss instigators. Most of my adult life I've tried to lose weight; most women have. The previous year I was on the Medifast diet with its low calorie meals, soups, pudding, shakes, protein bars and convenience of home delivery, cutting out any annoying trips to the grocery store. Even though the pounds were shedding fast, I always felt hungry and watched my hubby down his spare ribs and enchiladas as he once watched my Gazyva bag.

Unable to stay on Medifast, and with a death sentence of leukemia hanging over my head, I overindulged in food and screwed dying hungry. Late night binges alone became my modus operandi. A few Lay's potato chips, hell no, a whole bag. A Hershey's milk chocolate with almonds, hell no, three of them. A cup of Nalley's original chili, hell no, a whole can and with grated cheese on top to enhance its flavor. I was an eating machine who shoved common sense aside and stuffed whatever I wanted into my mouth. Suffice to say, I ballooned out over a few months and gained back every pound and more of the 35 I'd lost dieting. I was again officially designated OBESE on my doctor's chart in the section listed, *present medical conditions.*

Perhaps being without breasts and sporting a 10 inch scar across my face had a little something to do with my eating problem too. Acid reflux and nausea were now my diet partners and all I wanted was an ending to our relationship as soon as possible!

Wednesday morning, August 19th, came around and off again John and I traveled to WVCI. My appointment was at 8:15 am, with blood work the first thing on the agenda to make sure my neutrophil count was high enough for my Gazyva treatment. If neutrophil counts are too low then a person's body is too susceptible to infection and doctors will recommend waiting a day or two. Fortunately, my levels were maintained so my treatment schedule never altered.

Katy's twin, Jordan, was my nurse that day. She and Tracy were waiting for me as we walked into the treatment room and both looked a little stressed, but neither ever complained about anything. No talk of problems at home, heavy workloads, frustration among colleagues, or grumpy and difficult patients. Fighting cancer and making chemo as easy as possible on us victims always trumped any complaints they and those working alongside them might have had. They were professionals to a "T."

"How have you been?" asked Tracy, putting a smile on her pretty face as she found me a recliner with a nice window view. "Hope you were able to enjoy your days away from us."

"Well, I had one great nap and some good walks, and a nice time with the grandkids. Oh, and the patch worked real well. But acid reflux and nausea really got to me, so I didn't exactly ENJOY most of my days. I...."

"And she's hardly eating and what she does eat, comes back up," quickened John. "I'm really worried about her."

"Any chest pain, difficulty swallowing, or trouble sleeping at night?" Tracy rapid fired.

"No problem with the first two, but 'yes' to the third."

"I'm very sorry Pam and here's what we're going to do. First, we'll get you a prescription for Omeprazole that prevents the production of acid in your stomach and is used to treat gastroesophageal reflux disease, GERD. Eating is important to keep your energy level up so anything that interferes with food intake isn't good. If that doesn't work, we've got other things we can try."

"I read about what foods to avoid and what foods to eat and I'm sleeping with lots of pillows so my head is up high, more in a sitting position. I've had heartburn before, but nothing like this stuff."

"You're doing the right things, but I also want you to eat smaller meals and avoid eating late at night, okay?"

"That's easy. I hardly eat anything anyway," I forlorned.

"Well, we hope to change that soon," stated Tracy as Sarah took my vitals and Jordan began my pre-meds. I tried hard to de-stress as I listened to Tracy call in my new prescription, the one that'd have new side-effects all its own.

My girl was outside enjoying her morning in the sun, strolling across the pasture and checking the ground for a free meal. A bird landed and she taxied it over to the shade of her favorite oak tree. John helped cover me as usual in wonderfully warm blankets, and I turned my problems over to my team; I felt better.

"Alright if I take a look inside your mouth?' asked Tracy. "I want to check for any sores that could be developing; it's common for people undergoing chemo." She took out a small flashlight from her pocket and donned a pair of surgical gloves.

She found two small ones; one on my lower left gum and another on the roof of my mouth. No wonder my mouth felt icky. Acid reflux, nausea and now mouth sores. What next!

"I'm going to prescribe a special mouthwash; it's a combination of lidocaine to relieve pain, Mylanta which is an antacid that is a mucosal coating agent and Benadryl to reduce inflammation. Want you to use it every three to four hours by swishing it around in your mouth for one to two minutes and then spitting it out or swallowing it. Always shake the bottle before using and don't eat or drink for 30 minutes after use. It should help you start feeling better right away. It's called Magic Mouthwash," finished Tracy.

I chuckled at the name. "Well if it works, I don't care what it's called."

"I'll get a prescription into your pharmacy right now." She dialed the Safeway in Keizer and told me it'd be ready for pick up in a few hours. Then she continued with, "And suck on some hard candy, like Werther's Original Caramels, to help keep your mouth extra moist; that'll help too. Now I want to hear about your nausea."

"Well, it didn't come on until yesterday when I spent hours either throwing up or feeling like I was going to throw up. It was awful," I said.

"And the medication didn't help at all?" Tracy asked.

"No. Not at all."

"I'm going to add Zofran for your nausea. It dissolves on your tongue so you don't need to swallow it. Take the Zofran when you get home and keep taking it according to the directions."

"Should she take the other meds for nausea too?" queried my husband.

"No, take just the Zofran. And remember these meds are most effective to **prevent** problems, not after the fact.

My treatment with Gazyva started and all went fine, me taking a much needed nap, and John getting something to eat at a nearby restaurant. Shortly before our leaving, Tracy returned in hand with Omeprazole and Sharman's prescriptions for Zofran and the magical mouthwash. She also announced she'd arranged the days and times for my Neulasta shots at Dr. Strother's office in Salem. This girl had game and did what she said she'd do.

Our ride home was quiet and for good reason; we'd been to hell and back the last few days and talking would only sap our energy even more. Besides, we were always comfortable with silence between us. I was under the covers in my bedroom playing solitaire on my iPad when John returned with my prescriptions.

The directions on the bottle of Omeprazole said, 'Take one capsule by mouth one time daily. Swallow whole. Do not chew, crush or cut open capsule.' The English teacher in me noted that if the directions said to swallow whole, the chewing, crushing or opening was redundant. But then I figured the pharmacist knew his audience better than I did. A little yellow sticker added to the directions with, 'Take this medicine before a meal or as directed by your doctor. May cause DIZZINESS.'

The mouthwash side-effects could be a burning or tingling sensation in my mouth, drowsiness, constipation, diarrhea and nausea. Quite a smorgasbord of unique possibilities, none of which I even wanted to think about. I already had more than enough on my plate as it was.

Some of the side-effects of Zofran were diarrhea, headache, fever, dizziness, drowsiness, fast or pounding heartbeats, blurred vision... and I stopped right there. Enough was enough. I couldn't take anymore. "Hold on Rabbit, just hold on," was again my trial's mantra. I took my medicine like a good girl and waited to see if competing side-effects would get to me.

Lynne, my BFF, called later that afternoon and we had a good talk, about everything. She and I'd known each other since we were two years old, and if opposites attract then we were the classic example. I was a prude in school and she was a wild child. I remember one time when we were in college and she asked me to go to a party with her. Lynne spent a good share of the evening in a bedroom with a guy, and

I spent most of my time in the living room with another young man, removing his hands from my blouse buttons and stopping unwanted advances up my skirt. He told me he REALLY liked me and I was one of the prettiest girls he'd ever seen, as if that statement would put my boobs on display and open my legs. He even had the gall to announce, "You won't regret having sex with me; lots of girls have told me how great I am in bed." What a romantic!

"Guess that'll just be my loss," I remarked, followed by, "Get your God damn hands off me!" Talk about a "ME TOO" moment! It, along with 6 other sexual assaults during my lifetime, to this day really piss me off.

My best friend forever, Lynne never judges me or lies to me and she is loyal, not blindly loyal, but the good, seeing kind. I confide in her and never, ever do I worry that she'd betray my secrets. So what if she was a little loose with the male species, smoked cigarettes like a chimney and downed alcohol way too much. She is always there for me, and when I need her help, it's always given freely without a guilt trip attached. Her phone call helped me forget about my own troubles and avert a pathetic pity party.

I slept pretty well that night and the next, but when Friday the 21st came around, I was definitely in bad shape. Vomiting, or the urge to, took a back seat to another bout with acid reflux. We cancer patients in treatment are well-known for our coping abilities; we become masters of the cope, but I was failing the test miserably. Even with the Omeprazole and following Tracy's eating directions, I was in a world of hurt. A constant backwash of acid irritated my esophagus and it really, really hurt, overtaking the discomfort of mouth sores and any concerns about upchucking.

About all I could do was NOT eat or drink anything other than water, hoping such elimination of triggers would bring me sweet relief. So while I experimented with this unhealthy deprivation technique, instead of doing the smart thing and calling Tracy for more help, I searched the all powerful internet for GERD ideas. And guess what? People were posting about the curative power of apples, the fruit we all should eat every day anyway 'to keep the doctor away.'

So I left my computer and went downstairs and chomped on a Honeycrisp. In about a day's time I was much better and back to eating small meals. Maybe the medication had finally started to take effect, or the apple really worked; or once again, I **believed** the apple worked so it did; I don't really know for sure. But what I do know is I felt a heck of a lot better, and never again will I underestimate the curative power of Adam's downfall.

With the acid reflux problem going away, the mouth sores improving and the nausea situation getting under control, I still was a little 'off' and it wasn't other effects of my meds. It was something different; I could tell.

When Sunday, August 23rd arrived, I felt a little itchy, but thought it was caused by Charlie who'd recently put in a lot more than usual lap time. I shrugged off a small rash on my thighs; exactly the spot where my sweet feline sprawled himself when inside for the night. Then, much later that evening, I realized I was in a world of shit, shit that had absolutely nothing to do with acid reflux, nausea meds, or a cat named Charlie.

My body sported a red, scaly looking skin rash that covered my chest, back, bottom, thighs and knees. I quickly took my temperature; it was 100.4, exactly what I'd been warned as dangerous for people with leukemia and prone to infections. I immediately swallowed two extra strength 500mg of Tylenol, and started serious hydrating. My body itched like crazy, so I went downstairs to the utility room and stood in a cool shower while I re-ran in my mind the side-effects of Allopurinal. 'Rash and fever' stood out as some of the most prominent warnings.

I called the number Tracy had given me for emergencies and talked with an advice nurse who said I was doing all the right things. She instructed me to keep taking Tylenol and drink at least 16 ounces of water an hour; also, to continue taking my temperature every half hour and if it went up higher than 100.4, to quickly get myself to the nearest emergency room. And most importantly, STOP TAKING Allopurinal. "Jesus Christ!" I told myself.

It was midnight and time to wake up my poor husband who was already sleep- deprived from worrying about me. I went to his bedside and said, "John, I'm not feeling good."

He bolted upright and yelled, "What's wrong?"

"I've got a rash and a fever and feel terrible. Sorry."

I hurriedly explained everything to him, including the call to the advice nurse and my need for a trip to the ER if things worsened. He listened calmly during my talk, but was startled when he checked me out under the lights in the bathroom. "I've never seen anything like that," he said. "Does it itch?"

I nodded an emphatic 'Yes.'

"How long has it been since you took your temperature?"

"Close to a half hour," I answered.

"Well let's get you back in bed and take it again." He helped me lay down and then placed the thermometer under my tongue. Before long it beeped, registering my temperature at 100.2. Two tenths lower, not much but at least it was down a little and wasn't going up.

The rest of the night was spent cooling my body with cold showers, drinking lots of Smart Water, resting and taking my temperature every 30 minutes. At 8:00 am the next morning, Monday, August 24th, I called Tracy and left a message, hoping to catch her before she started her rounds. I also made darn sure I did not take my usual morning dosage of Allopurinal. Ten minutes later she called and cut to the chase.

"Pam, I want you to get here as soon as you can. Dr. Sharman isn't in today, but his nurse practioner, Pat, is and I've brought her up to speed on what's happening. When can you come?"

I looked at John who'd been listening in on our conversation and he shouted, "Seventy minutes!"

"Great," Tracy replied. "Check in at the front desk and after your blood draw, we'll call you back. Keep drinking water in the car and try not to worry. And don't take any more Allopurinal."

"I'm never taking it again," was my reply.

We threw on our clothes, backed the car out of the garage, and drove the 64 miles in record time. I found myself sitting in an exam room at 9:15 am. Pat and Tracy carefully examined my ugly rash, both of them sporting astonished looks on their faces. Tracy took my temperature, checked my blood pressure and pulse rate, and made sure my oxygen levels were within normal range. Pat, after a quick introduction, checked my lungs and examined the lymph nodes in my neck, arm pits and groin areas. Afterwards she sat impatiently in front of her computer awaiting the results of my blood tests. The side-effects of Allopurinal were serious business.

The computer screen finally lit up with my CBC (Complete Blood Count) results and Pat told me and John that things, "Looked good." But with no time to enjoy the news, she went on to the scary reality of sepsis, a potentially life-threatening complication of infections among people like me with a weakened immune system. Sepsis can turn severe and lead to septic shock, followed by death. The medical community made it clear people don't always die because of their diseases; they often die because of the results of their treatment. Clinical trial patients can be among those if they're not careful.

"You're very lucky, Pam. Very lucky. Not only did you experience serious side effects of Allopurinal, but your high fever indicated some kind of infection. Remember, any fever of 100.4 or higher is a signal to get help immediately, and I mean IMMEDIATELY!"

My eyes teared up and she lowered her voice. "Don't get me wrong, it was good you called the Advice Nurse and took Tylenol and did extra hydration, but from now on, please, also go to the ER. They can start IV fluids and get you on medication that'll make sure you won't go into sepsis. Okay?"

"Yes," I apologized, followed quickly by John's "Sorry." Tracy walked over and gave me a big hug and smiled at the Squirrel.

"The main thing is you're going to be fine," said Tracy. "What you did brought your fever down and you got here quickly. And you know exactly what to do if something like this ever happens again."

"For sure," said John, looking restless and ready to head back toward Keizer, getting his Rabbit safely in her nest.

"Before you leave, here's a prescription for Methylprednisolone," said Pat, handing me a piece of paper. "I want you to pick it up at our pharmacy and take the first dosage right away; don't wait until you get home. It's a corticosteroid that treats inflammation of the skin and should take care of that rash. And here's a second prescription; it's an antibiotic, Cephalexin. It'll take care of any infection the Allopurinal might have caused. Take it right away too. Also, keep drinking lots of water and monitor your temperature every couple of hours. If anything, and I mean ANYTHING comes up, call right away. Got it?"

"Got it," we answered in unison.

"And I'll see you on Wednesday morning, 8:00 am sharp," Tracy reminded me while thumbing through to the treatment schedule of the growing folder labeled 'Pamela Corinne Johnson, BG Trial.'

"See you then," John told her as he guided me out the door to the pharmacy. It took only a few minutes to get the Methylprednisolone and Cephalexin and as I downed the pills, a wave of relief spread over me. Soon the nasty rash would be one more side-effect of treatment that'd be a thing of the past. Adding these two new drugs to the ones I already had sitting on my dresser at home, I figured the total number was about 10. And that wasn't even counting the Bendamustine, Gazyva and all my pre-meds. I felt like a walking, talking, pharmacy.

We arrived home well before noon. I finished what was left of my water bottle, peed about a quart and feeling a little cold and a lot tired, slid under the covers of my bed once more and went to sleep. I woke up a couple hours later to John making big labels for all my medications and lining bottles up on my dresser like GI Joe's in marching formation ready to do battle.

Over-the-counter stuff like Tylenol, Ibuprofen, and Claritin were on the far left end, and to the right of them were my nausea meds, Prochlorperazine, Lorazepam and my lovely Zofran (Ondansetron) orally disintegrating tablets. Next was my Omeprazole for acid reflux, with my Magic Mouthwash stored in the refrigerator. Finishing up the formation were my new recruits to battle my recent rash and infection, Methylprednisolone and Cephalexin. Johnny attached large post-it notes to my pill bottles, writing the intent of each med, and he also wrote out a big time table for their taking and taped it to my large bedroom mirror which hung above the line of containers. Squirrel had turned my mess of meds into prescriptions I could easily distinguish and he also showed me precisely when they needed giving. My husband had come to the rescue again.

Tuesday rolled around and the grandkids had the sniffles so they postponed their visit. We really missed them, but couldn't chance picking up any germs, especially at this stage of the trial. I was more than bummed out, but talked with Karin like I did almost daily and found out she wanted to take me to my last August treatment before her school year started at Battle Creek Elementary. Part of me wanted her to, but the other part didn't want her to see the stark reality of chemotherapy; the hospital smell of the treatment room, nurses trying to find good veins in arms bruised by previous attempts, skinny, pale patients under blankets with stocking caps covering bald heads and the incessant beeping of machines. And the worst thing, Karin would be watching ME, her mom, sit in a chair with intravenous drugs flowing into my body just like everyone else. Yes, I was just like everyone else... we're all like everyone else.

"How about a walk down to the river and back and then I'll get you a Pomegranate Paradise at Jamba Juice?" asked my hubby, bringing me back to the here and now.

My first inclination was to say no and feel sorry for myself because the Monekes couldn't come over, but that wouldn't have helped anybody, especially the man I loved. "Sounds good to me," I exclaimed, avoiding a giant FUBAR.

John's eyes spoke of relief when he came back with, "Great!"

The walk down Shoreline Avenue to Sunset Park definitely improved my mood. Wind rustled the leaves on Birch and Dogwood trees along the way, and baskets of flowers hung from every home's front porch. Yards had turned brown from the hot summer, even as sprinklers watered them in their attempt for revival. Once at the Willamette, we skipped rocks; my best was five, while John didn't cut me any slack with his eight. The river's current was slow, and ducks and geese floated along for the ride. I walked over to a tall fir tree, stripped some needles from a branch and rubbed them between my fingers and brought them up to my nose. They smelled like they always did, Christmas.

"How you doing, Rabbit?" my first place competitor asked.

"Not bad, but I think I'm ready for that Jamba. Oh, and Karin wants to take me to chemo tomorrow," I stated rather abruptly.

He furrowed his brow and asked, "Sure you're alright with that? You know I like being with you during your treatments."

"I know, Honey. But she wants to do more for me, and for you too. And after thinking about it, spending time together tomorrow might be good...for both of us. So what do you think?"

"I think you're probably right."

We strolled back home and I plopped on the loveseat in the TV room where John had keyed up my favorite scene from THE RIGHT STUFF, a movie about the US space program in its early infancy and the seven Mercury astronauts who were an important part of it. I loved watching Gordon (Gordo) Cooper played by Dennis Quaid cruise down the road towards Edwards Air Force Base in California, with rockabilly singer Jimmy Lloyd's, 'I Got a Rocket in my Pocket', blaring on his radio. The melody is pure country rock'n roll and every time I hear it I get a grin on my face almost as wide as Quaid's. It's definitely a "feel good" movie, the best kind of film to watch during a person's part time job to beat cancer.

"Thanks, honey!" I yelled as he headed out the door toward my Paradise. What could have been a pretty lousy day and evening had detoured into one of my best.

Karin was over by 6:30 am, Wednesday, August 27th, and we drove to WVCI as the sun slowly rose over the hills from the East. My horse was already grazing in the field, and I pointed her out to my daughter as we neared the clinic's big parking lot.

"So that's the one you've been telling us all about, Mom. She's a lot bigger than I pictured her."

"She's there every day. We all watch her out the window, even the nurses and doctors. No one seems to know her name though. One nurse's aide said she's been in that field for years."

"Is she always alone?" asked Karin, sadness in her voice.

"I've seen a girl with her sometimes, petting and grooming her or giving her fresh water and food, but mostly when I'm here she's alone. Oh, and I've seen people walk by her fence, call her over and give her apples and carrots."

"Maybe you can too."

"Maybe," I replied.

After checking in at reception, Karin marched by my side into the treatment room where I selected a chair with a nice view of the lawns surrounding the building, my horse and in close proximity to my favorite bathroom. She slid a nearby chair up close to mine, sat down, and nervously eyed her surroundings.

"So this is it," she whispered.

"Yep, this is it," I said as Sarah quickly took my temperature, blood pressure and pulse, and as always, checked my oxygen content.

"Everything's normal, Pam."

"That's always good," I told her and then added. "This is my daughter Karin." Sarah smiled and said a quick hello before being called away to check on another patient.

"Well, the last treatment for August," Tracy said as she welcomed me with her usual friendliness. "And how is your rash?"

"Slowly fading away," I exclaimed. "And almost no more itching either."

"That's what we like to hear," she said as she read over the vitals Sarah had recorded on my chart. "And who is this with you today instead of John?"

"Karin, my daughter; I've told you a lot about her."

"Yes, sure," said Tracy, definite recognition in her voice. "I'm very glad to meet you."

Karin held out her hand and returned the greeting. "Mom's told us all about you and everything you've done for her. Thanks for your help."

"You're very welcome," Tracy replied. "Your mom is doing great,

Karin. She's handled the side-effects well and hopefully from now on they'll get less and less." She then turned her gaze toward me when Katy arrived with premeds and finished with, "Well, looks like we're ready to start."

"Let's do it," I said with conviction.

Karin carefully observed as Katy sprayed my port with the cold numbing agent and then inserted the needle for the half hour of premeds. When I shivered, Karin knew exactly where the warm blankets were and covered me from chin to toes. She placed my bottled water on the chair's shelf, unscrewed the lid and motioned for me to start hydrating.

Thirty minutes later I unplugged my machine and walked to and from the bathroom with Karin navigating the trip through the crowded treatment room. Again in the recliner, Sarah took my vitals and Katy started the Gazyva, my single drug of the day. I looked at my daughter and she looked at me.

"How are you doing, Mom?"

"Fine, Pumpkin. Really, I'm fine," I said with reassurance.

"Can I get you anything? Anything to help you?" she pleaded.

"Well," I paused. "Why don't you read me some of that book you brought today. The one you love and are having your students read again this year."

"Sure," she said, happy to answer my request. And she began reading WONDER, the New York Times bestseller by R. J. Palacio. Its story is about Auggie, a 5th grade boy who has a rare facial deformity and is ostracized and bullied at school before finally being accepted for the **wonder full** person he is.

Karin took the book from her large bag and opened to the first chapter. I settled back in my chair and listened carefully to my daughter's sweet voice as she read the first section of WONDER. It was titled, 'Ordinary.'

I know I'm not an ordinary ten-year-old kid. I mean, sure I do ordinary things. I eat ice cream. I ride my bike. I play ball. I have an XBOX. Stuff like that makes me ordinary. I guess. And I feel ordinary.

Inside. But I know ordinary kids don't make other ordinary kids run away screaming in playgrounds. I know ordinary kids don't get stared at wherever they go.

If I found a magic lamp and I could have one wish, I would wish that I had a normal face that no one ever noticed at all. I would wish that I could walk down the street without people seeing me and then doing that look-away thing. Here's what I think: the only reason I'm not ordinary is that no one else sees me that way.

But I'm kind of used to how I look by now. I know how to pretend I don't see the faces people make. We've all gotten pretty good at that sort of thing: me, Mom and Dad, Via. Actually, I take that back: Via's not so good at it. She can get really annoyed when people do something rude. Like, for instance, one time in the playground some older kids made some noises. I don't even know what the noises were exactly because I didn't hear them myself, but Via heard and she just started yelling at the kids. That's the way she is. I'm not that way.

Via doesn't see me as ordinary. She says she does, but if I were ordinary, she wouldn't feel like she needs to protect me as much.

And Mom and Dad don't see me as ordinary, either. They see me as extraordinary. I think the only person in the world who realizes how ordinary I am is me.

My name is August, by the way. I won't describe what I look like. Whatever you're thinking, it's probably worse.

As she paused before reading the next section, I noticed patients on either side of us were also listening to Auggie's story. The curly-haired blond woman on my left who was having a blood transfusion leaned toward Karin and asked, "If you don't mind me asking, what's the name of that book?"

"It's WONDER by R. J. Palacio. I use it in my 4th grade classroom," my daughter replied.

The man reclining on my right, whose wife had put down her AARP magazine when she first heard Karin's voice, said, "I think our grandson would really like that book. I heard about it from our neighbor, but with this chemo stuff for my prostate, neither of us has thought of much else."

"Know exactly what you mean," I chimed in.

Karin continued reading sections of WONDER; the sound of her voice, always calm and gentle. I easily pictured Auggie, his sister Via, his mom and dad, his teachers and his different schoolmates, even his dog. The story and its reader captured me completely.

The time for flushing my port came sooner than expected, as Katy quickly unhooked the empty bag of Gazyva. Tracy checked my vitals before handing me my next appointment card with September 9th and 10th written on it. She pointed out that both Gazyva and Bendamustine would be given on Wednesday the 9th, so it'd be a longer day than when Benda was only administered on the 10th. Then she said, "I've arranged with Salem Hemotology for your Neulasta shot at 3:00 pm on the 11th."

"You're my guardian angel; hope you know that," I told her. "Don't know what I'd do without you."

Turning a bit red in the face, she replied, "We all just want to help you, Pam." After a deep sigh she continued, "Karin, it was wonderful to meet you. Your mom is one special lady."

Karin smiled and agreed, "Yes, she is."

Tracy took the blankets from us while Karin slid the small tray back under the arm of the recliner, and I drank the remainder of my water. Then my daughter handed me the book she had shared and said it was mine. Inside, on the very first page she had inscribed—

> Mom—
> I hope you love
> this book as much
> as I do! Thank you for
> being my **Wonder** Woman!
> I love you!
> KC
> 8/26/15

We walked to the car holding hands, just like we used to do when she was young and I was younger. I remember thinking on our drive home that this clinical trial wasn't so bad after all, and maybe the worst was over. My acid reflux was gone, nausea and vomiting almost a thing of the past, mouth sores healing nicely and the terrible rash of Allopurinol, fading more with each passing day. "Knock on wood; I was feeling pretty darn good."

Karin hummed softly in the seat next to me, her 'tell' that she was relaxed and in a happy mood. I thought about talking with her about our day, but decided otherwise, judging that our being together spoke enough for us.

After many drafts and careful revisions of a group email to family and friends summarizing my clinical trial adventures thus far, I pushed the Send button on my computer. It felt good to end a revisiting of all that had happened.

So the first month of my six month part time job had come to a close. August's treatments were done, each with their own awful side effects, and now I had ten more sessions to work my way through. With continued comfort from an old horse, warm blankets, good pokes, and family and friends, I had little doubt I'd make it to the finish line in my trial against CLL. Being the 'glass is half full kind of gal,' I believed the worst was behind me, but little did I expect what September would bring.

SEPTEMBER SURPRISE

On September 5th, Karin dropped off the grandkids for a visit; they both had something special for me. Sydney's gift was a tiny Lego warrior woman she'd put together. It had a helmet of gold, body fitting armor and in one hand held a long sword and in the other, a shield decorated with a flying horse. Syd said I was a brave woman, even braver than the warrior. Her younger brother Aiden had also assembled something for me, a Lego kitty that was black and white like my sweet Charlie. Aiden said I should put it in my purse because, "You always carry your purse around with you and the real Charlie is too big to fit in it." I looked at these two little kids with love sparkling in their eyes and I almost lost it.

We played for a while in our backyard; the four of us bopping a balloon around and making sandcastles on Johnsons' Beach. And before they left, Grandpa made everyone giant snow cones covered in grape syrup. It was a wonderful two hours, the best a grandma could ever want.

Sometimes I wonder if the memories I have of special moments are the same others will recall someday. "Will Sydney and Aiden REMEMBER the tiny Legos they made me? Will they remember the big beach in our backyard, summers at Neskowin and how much I loved them?" My grandchildren fill up every part of my being; will I fill up a little part of their being after I'm gone? And will their recollections of the good far outweigh the bad?

I know all too well that as an adult I have specific memories of my childhood, but sadly many of the most vivid ones aren't happy. This doesn't mean I had terrible parents or evil sisters who made my middle position a difficult one. It simply means the negative in our lives has a great capacity to darken the positive. Thinking about all this reminded me of a Countee Cullen poem entitled, "Incident," that I first read while being the only white student enrolled in a class called 'Black Poetry' at the University of Oregon.

INCIDENT

Once riding in old Baltimore,
Heart-filled, head –filled with glee,
I saw a Baltimorean
Keep looking straight at me.

Now I was eight and very small,
And he was no whit bigger,
And so I smiled, but he poked out
His tongue, and called me, 'Nigger.'

I saw the whole of Baltimore
From May until December,
Of all the things that happened there
That's all that I remember.

Sunday, the 6th, was pretty uneventful although my scalp started itching, terribly. Scratching my head as if it were covered in busy lice didn't offer any relief and only resulted in shoulders covered by snow-like pieces of dried skin. John, bless his squirrel heart, went to the store at my urgent request and brought home the best moisturizing shampoo and conditioner he could find, and luckily, after multiple washings in the shower, my scalp was soothed a little.

Then while toweling off in front of the bathroom mirror, I took careful stock of my aging body and immediately noticed that my arms, legs, chest, fanny, back, hands and feet were extremely dry. They didn't itch and certainly didn't resemble the scale-like rash of Allopurinal, but when I sampled a scratch of my body and eyebrows, the irritated epidermis drifted like snowflakes onto the light blue rug beneath my bare feet. My face and neck were the lone regions void of this new side-effect of chemo. Without hesitation, I dialed Tracy's cell and she answered before the third ring. I explained the situation and she came back with unexpected advice.

"After every shower and bath, I want you to apply olive oil over your w-h-o-l-e body. Doesn't matter if it's extra-virgin or just the regular kind. It'll help with the dry skin problem right away. Patients going through chemotherapy swear by it," she said.

"You mean, the olive oil I use to cook with; the stuff I buy at Safeway to fry chicken in?" I asked in disbelief.

"Yes, that's it exactly," she answered.

"Well.....okay, if you say so, if you're sure."

"And start taking Vitamin B. That should help too. Oh, and some patients have used a thick cream called Eucerin, but it's kind of expensive, so if I were you, I'd use the olive oil," was her learned opinion.

I had some Vitamin B in the medicine cabinet so took one right away and then headed to the kitchen to check on our stock of olive oil; we had a couple big bottles of STAR, with the phrase, "A key to good health since 1898," advertised on the side. I took that to mean taken internally and not rubbed over my body, but maybe the company knew a whole lot more than I did about the side-effects of a CLL clinical trial. I lathered up like a greased pig at a rodeo and in no time at all, my skin returned to normal.

On Monday we were greeted again by September sunshine, so John and I went to Bush Park tennis courts to hit some balls. I hadn't played in months because of my enlarged 'Billie Jean Spleen' so John made sure every ball he hit landed within 3 steps of me, all of them minus

his usual power and brutal topspin. After a while, muscle memory returned and my form and consistency improved. I started hitting the
ball deeper on his side of the court and feeling like I could be a tennis
player again.

Things were going well for 30 minutes, but then they turned bad. I
lost steam like a train going up- hill, and I barely made it to the shade
and nearby bench on the side of the court.

"Are you okay?" asked my worried husband.

"Not really," I replied with a strange sounding cough. "Think it's
time to go home." My face was turning pale and I could feel myself get
dizzy.

John gathered up our tennis gear and gestured for me to drink my
bottle of water, all of it, while we sat on the bench longer. "Bet you're
dehydrated. Shouldn't have let you hit for so long."

"No, it's my fault. I start to feel good and think I'm back to being Pam
again when really I'm not yet. When will I ever learn!"

"You'll get there, Rabbit." He leaned over and gave me a peck on the
forehead. "Right now, let's get you home."

We walked back to the car, my husband with two tennis bags slung
over his left shoulder and me watching my feet so I wouldn't trip on
the uneven path. Once there, he turned the air conditioning on 'high'
and tilted my seat all the way back. I breathed deeply, drank the rest
of his water and tried my best to picture Syd and Aiden playing on our
beach. Luckily, half way home the dizziness and weakness let up, but
my throat was still dry even with all the water I'd downed. "Strange,"
I thought. Crawling into bed, I slept most of the remainder of the day,
finally waking up as it was just starting to get dark outside.

Chemo was scheduled for Wednesday the 9th at 7:45 am, with infusions of both Gazyva and Bendamustine; Thurday the 10th at 9:00
am, with just Bendamustine. Then on Friday I'd get my Neulasta shot
at 2:15 pm at Salem Hospital's hematology/oncology department. September was nicely planned.

On Wednesday things went pretty smoothly with all the ups and
downs of August behind me. My infection fighting neutrophils were

again holding nicely, and what once seemed long ago, the foreign adversary of the treatment area, was now my comrade in arms.

Tracy visited as usual to check on me and I told her about my hoarse cough and dry mouth. Right away she advised more hydration, brushing my teeth 4 times daily with Biotene toothpaste partnered with its spray or gel especially at bedtime, and sucking more often on hard candy. Werther's, Honey Crisps, olive oil, and now Biotene, I never thought those things would become such an important part of my clinical trial care.

On Thursday as we drove to the WVCI parking structure; there was my pretty girl in her field as always, more and more a dependable buddy I could count on. We stared intently at one another and for the briefest of moments, made a small connection. Once in my recliner, the pre-meds made their way into my veins and I read a new saying written on the treatment windows. It was by Allison A. and said, "Scars may heal, blood counts may normalize, years may pass. But never again will the simple act of waking up to a normal, boring day as a healthy individual be taken for granted, nor go unappreciated." Truer words were never spoken.

The 'going well' of that day suddenly stopped when Tracy told us she was leaving her job as clinical trial nurse to take a different position elsewhere. She'd been working for a long time helping people like me and the stress, long hours, and burden of fighting cancer had taken a huge toll on both her and her young family. She simply couldn't do it anymore. I felt abandoned; I was losing my guardian angel. It was all I could do to hold it together and not burst into tears. First Betty and now, Tracy.

"You'll be in excellent hands with Shawna," she gently reassured me, coming closer and touching my arm. "Her patients love her and she's been brought up to speed with everything about you. I've asked her to come by in a little while to meet you and John." Tracy paused and looked hard at me. "I hope you understand," she added.

"I do understand. Don't worry," I whispered with forgiveness. Still, things seemed to be forever changing and causing uncertainty and this propelled my fears. At least my horse was still with me... my sweet 4-legged comfort in a scary whirlwind of newness.

With the pre-meds finished and Sarah having completed the taking of my usual set of vitals, Katy started the Gazyva around 10:00 am. Tracy excused herself to begin her rounds with other patients and tell them what I'd just been told, that she was leaving. I hadn't been in the mood for much more than a cup of Yoplait before we'd left home that morning, so John handed me the fresh peach and Graham Crackers he'd packed. For some reason a peach seemed more like a celebration of good news so I decided on the crackers. Starting on my third Graham a chipper, young voice joined my treatment area.

"Hello, Pam. I'm Shawna and I'm taking over as your clinical trial nurse." John and I looked intently at the pretty young lady with dark rimmed glasses, flawless complexion, and petite frame who clutched my ever growing CLL file. Before sitting down in the chair beside us, she warmly greeted George, another patient nearby who looked to be in his eighties.

"How you doing today?" she asked him.

"About as well as to be expected, I guess. What's the phrase nowadays? Oh yea, 'It is what it is,'" George answered his own question.

"I'll be over in just a little bit and we'll have a good talk," said Shawna.

"Sounds good," said the old man. "I'll be here." Sarah covered him in a warm blanket and put apple juice and Saltines on his tray. "Thank you, dear," he said sweetly before closing his eyes.

"Tracy's on her way back and will join us soon," said Shawna, bringing us back to our conversation. She slowly broke the ice with information about her background as a trial nurse, a few tidbits about her personal life, and a couple simple health questions for me. She settled in naturally, completely in tune with all that was going on around her. John noticed it too.

When Tracy arrived, they nodded at one another and then turned their attention to me and my hubby. They explained the routine handoff of a patient from one clinical trial nurse to another and promised me uninterrupted care. As they spoke more and more about this changing of the guard, my worries eased a bit, and although I still didn't like what was happening, I accepted it more as the norm in medicine rather than the exception. "It is what it is," as George said.

On Friday John and I drove to Salem Hospital where I received, not a patch, but my first Neulasta shot. We sat in the waiting room for 15 minutes while the refrigerated serum warmed up to room temperature and I wrote the receptionist a co-pay check for $367.86. When called back to the treatment room I was met by a solemn lab assistant with a big needle and a cotton ball dipped in alcohol. He did his business slowly and without small talk, and then off Squirrel and I went for a late lunch at the Applebee's close to home.

That weekend and a few days following, I dusted around the house, did loads of laundry, read, wrote in my journal, gave John long back-rubs and Charlie lots of pets, shopped for groceries at Safeway, cooked dinners, and spent precious hours with Karin, Sydney and Aiden. I enjoyed all free of side-effects, a huge step forward for month 2 of my clinical trial. Losing Tracy and finding Shawna didn't seem so tragic anymore.

On September 17th, John headed to Yakima, Washington, for his tennis team's mixed doubles sectional competition, and I was glad to see him go. My cancer and its treatment had taken a front seat to his needs and wants, and it was well beyond time for him to get away from the battle I was waging. He was paired up with a strong lady player who possessed fast twitch muscles, a great set of wheels, and never-ending stamina, three things terribly lacking in his wife with CLL.

In our younger years, John and I won so many tournaments our separate trophy collections were outrageous, and once we joined forces as partners the collection multiplied like rabbits in heat. Statues and plaques were a sweet trip down memory lane, but now as we grew older, our priorities shifted. We both agreed that being in the present was much more worthwhile than basking in our past days of glory. A few years ago we answered the call to donate our trophies to the YMCA and today have only three as a reminder of how we once struck fear in many an opponents' eyes.

With John in Washington and me feeling good about my CLL part time job situation, I got the overpowering urge to beautify our yard. As most people know, urges can be very strange things. They can come over a person suddenly or in my case, come to the surface again and again until the call to action is finally too powerful for resistance...and with my hubby absent, my loving resistance was on the tennis courts in the nearby Evergreen State. So it was the perfect storm; a communion of my love to take something ugly and make it beautiful, and the unrestrained freedom to do so.

With no thought to being in a clinical trial for leukemia, I set forth to take out the grass in our front and back yard. I figured my trusty spade and I could handle the job slowly and surely; after all, I'd done a good share of removal to increase the square footage of our beach only a few years ago. Sod was sod, not cement for heaven's sake.

John was barely out of the driveway when I plunged the shovel into the grass, expecting great success and easy exit of my first big chunk of green. Unfortunately, it was much more difficult than anticipated, yet 4 hours later I managed another 50 to 60 shovelfuls. The problem though became pretty evident; I'd bitten off a hell of a lot more than I could chew. Taking out even a small lawn, not piecemeal like making a beach over years and years, was a task for serious machinery, not a single spade and a determined woman with an urge.

My arms ached, my back ached, my legs ached, everything ached, but it felt fantastic to be doing something other than dealing with leukemia. Besides, working in my yard was the WELL PAM of me, not the SICK PAM of me. I retreated inside and googled landscape companies in Salem, Oregon.

After time well spent at the computer, I settled on Greer Brothers Landscaping, a company serving the area since 1946, one that promised 'quality at an affordable price.' They also gave free estimates and had excellent customer reviews. Even better, they could come out in just a few days, not weeks, to look over the job. In the mean time, I could purchase different ornamental grasses, step-ables and feather rock in place of lawn for the front, and look forward to a much more level yard in the back with grass better suited to weather in the Pacific Northwest. Our yard would improve her looks, be a thing of year-round beauty, and out every window of our home, a picture worth the making.

That evening I soaked my tired bones in the bathtub and noticed a tight feeling around my port area; not painful, more weird than anything else. Of course my whole body had been feeling DIFFERENT for a long time. Breasts cut off, CLL and its discomforts, Merkel skin cancer, clinical trial, and all the little stuff in between. I was pretty used to the unusual, so 'a little out of the ordinary' was put aside.

Karin kept me company with a sleep-over the next night, Friday, September 18th, and since Squirrel was out of town with his tennis buds, I was more than grateful for the company of my sweet daughter. Karin and I are easy together, like a pair of comfy slippers or sweat bottoms that relax in all the right places. Like most mothers and daughters we have a shared history and the years when it was just the two of us, we faced the world head on and were one another's saving grace. When John joined our twosome, he helped us find our smiles, and now 30 years later, we're closer than we've ever been.

KC arrived around 5:00 o'clock and we went out for a quick bite at our favorite Mexican restaurant, Los dos Hermanos. We loved the place and like Neskowin on the Oregon Coast, it housed memories of many celebrations... birthdays, graduations, Mother and Father's Day, anniversaries and lots of other milestones. It was our perfect **gathering** place.

Back home, Charlie snuggled on my lap for his usual rub and Karin settled underneath a soft blanket on the sofa as we watched a slew of silly sitcoms, avoiding anything unhappy or overly serious. My clinical trial had already been enough trauma and drama, and there was no reason to add to it that night.

"How ya doing, Mama?" Karin asked, calling me by my favorite term of endearment.

"Great! Got my daughter here for a sleep-over and I'm in my happy place."

We smiled at each other and as her gaze returned to the TV, she looked exactly like I remembered her in first grade, a little girl with the cutest profile of high cheek bones, rounded nose and tiny chin. It had been a teaching day for her at the end of a busy week, so we went to bed early, with us sleeping side by side. We talked just a little, but those things will remain private, and she dozed off with me listening to the rhythm of her breathing. Here we were together again, like we'd oftentimes been after her father left. All those years in between suddenly slipped away; she was my little girl, but I wasn't young; I was still an old woman with leukemia. "Damn," I said to myself, feeling again that little twinge by my port.

Both Syd and Aiden had early morning soccer matches the next day, so Karin hurried back to get them in uniform, fed and out the door so Drew could be on the fields before any of his players. He relished his role as 'Coach Moneke' and all the kids and parents loved him. He was just the kind of manly role model everyone respected, not the "winning is everything" kind of guy whose ego is wrapped up in making himself bigger by making others smaller. He was a teacher of the sport of soccer- kind, fair, knowledgeable and always set a good example for others. Talk about me seeing a glass as half full, he saw empty ones as vessels awaiting overflow.

Karin and I sat together on the sideline for the kiddos' games and cheered everyone on. Aiden's team, with daddy as coach, worked their little hearts out and in the second half when an opponent went down hard on the grass, tripping himself while dribbling, my grandson jogged over to help the player up and make sure he was alright.

Most parents clapped for Aiden's sweet display of a little boy's sportsmanship, but a nearby voice hollered, "Hey kid, don't do that! Get back on defense!" I gave the gentleman my best stink eye and said, "That's my grandson you just yelled at." He returned my gaze, but realized there was no way he could come out on top of what he'd started, so with sure footed swiftness, he moved his fold up chair and walked far, far away. Fortunately, Karin and Syd had been visiting the port-a-potty while this was going on and been spared the guy's disparaging remarks and my grandmotherly retort.

Syd's soccer game followed a short time later, and they were up against girls who looked much older, at least 4th graders who were a lot bigger and taller. Sydney was especially happy because she was goalie for part of the game, something she really liked as a change from her usual center forward spot. As balls whizzed straight for her, she trapped them on the ground, putting her small body in harm's way to make sure she stopped any possibility of a score. There was my little grand-daughter, cheeks bright red from exertion and with the 'eye of the tiger' determination in every ounce of her being. Like Jake Gleeson, Syd's Portland Timbers' hero, she and her teammates had put their all into every play and left everything they had on the field when the final whistle blew.

Skill and heart won out over size that day as her team celebrated with their usual holding of hands in a long line and running across the field to thank all their supporters for coming. Then came, like with Aiden's team's earlier, the handing out of individual 'treat bags' put together by the parents. This time they were filled with protein bars, Halo oranges, chips, a cookie and miniature sized Three Musketeers and to drink, Gatorade or Capri Sun for the asking. Extra bags were available too should a younger brother or sister be overcome with grief because they'd been left out, regardless of the fact they hadn't set foot on the playing field.

Neither Karin nor I knew for sure what the final score was, only that our team had made more goals than the other. Winning mattered, but it wasn't the end all; playing one's best was more important, that and always being a good sport. Drew stressed this as a coach and the kids understood these life- long lessons better than a good share of the parents.

The next day I sat at the computer and sent out another clinical trial update to family and friends. Many had been calling and were concerned they hadn't heard from me for a while. I didn't want to forget that they needed reassurance that I was doing okay and hadn't kicked the bucket.

Hello Everyone. Wanted to give you another update regarding the clinical trial I am taking part in to treat my Chronic Lymphocytic Leukemia, CLL. I had treatments number 6 and 7 two weeks ago at the Willamette Valley Research Center in nearby Springfield, Oregon. Blood work shows that my cancer cells continue to decrease with the infusion of the combined drugs, Gazyva and Bendamustine, and that's wonderful. I'm over my rash and haven't had a fever for almost a month. As the treatments continue, I can feel myself getting more easily fatigued at times, but at other times I pretty much feel like my old self. Occasionally, I still have to pop some pills so I won't vomit, but I'm getting accustomed to that being part of my new normal. Iron levels are going down, but recent tests and the expertise of my oncologist both confirmed this is most likely caused by the drugs and not any type of internal bleeding. I've had 2 Neulasta shots to "tell" my bone marrow to produce healthy lymphocytes after each chemo cycle and I'm now starting to feel some bone and joint pain, but it's manageable.

John and Karin are my amazing support system every step of the way and I love them VERY much. October 7-8 will be my next chemo days, with Neulasta on the 9th. Then I'll be half way through all this. Went for a walk with John this morning at Minto Island and marveled at the cloud formations and a huge blue heron gliding over head, not to mention all the happy dogs running free. There is so much to be thankful for and I'm very thankful you are in my life. Take care and much love to all of you. Pam

John did super at sectionals, winning 3 out of 3 matches, and arrived home on Sunday, the 20th. With great glee I explained my lawn project, and he didn't dampen my enthusiasm with cost projections and other practical matters. On the 23rd an employee of Greer Brothers came over and together we decided what would be best for both the front and back yard and the cost was more than affordable. Finally, my desire for a picture perfect yard would come to fruition; I was one happy gardener, and John was happy I was happy.

We drove to Al's Nursery in Woodburn, a quick 20 minutes from our home and bought ornamental grasses and lots of blooming ground cover that would look good next to the two dry river beds planned for the front. I had a project to look forward to, that little tightness next to my clavicle was hardly noticeable, and within days strong men would be taking out our tired, brown and dying old lawn that'd been an eyesore for more years than I cared to remember. Life was on the upswing!

Thursday morning arrived and I was at my dermatologist Dr. Carolyn Hale's office for my routine skin exam. Ever since my Merkel diagnosis I'd been coming in every 3 months to check for all kinds of abnormalities and skin cancers such as basal and squamous cell carcinoma, melanoma, and of course a recurrence of the dreaded one with the capital "M." Unlike the skin I enjoyed in my youth, free of moles, liver spots and all the other unnatural looking things, I was now head over heels covered in all sorts of strange spots and areas ripe for close examination by Hale.

Standing with only my Bali panties on in front of her and a nice nurse at a laptop who was documenting the exam and comparing it to my last visit, I was long past female modesty. If full exposure resulted in catching skin cancers early, being in the buff was a small price to pay. The exam was going well, no new areas of concern or dire need for biopsies, when suddenly she zeroed in on my left arm and, SURPRISE! A routine exam turned into a life and death matter. "How long has this purple blotchiness been here?" she asked with alarm in her voice.

"I don't know," I managed to answer. "This is the first time I've noticed it."

Dr. Hale quickly took my pulse in my left wrist and noticed again that my port had been placed in my left clavicle area. Right away I remembered just a couple days ago thinking, "tightness, hardly noticeable." Could this have been a warning sign, just like that pea-sized lump in my breast years ago, or cyst-like lump on my cheek, or heightened lymphocyte numbers during a yearly physical?

The doctor gently turned my arm to look at the inside by the elbow and also examined under my armpit. "I want you to call your clinical trial nurse or doctor as soon as you get home in case you have a blood clot, Pam. Your pulse is normal; however, the purple coloring means blood flow is being restricted somewhere. I'm sorry, but this needs to be addressed immediately."

Whispered under my breath so as not to scare the other lady in the room, I said my favorite cuss words, "SHIT!" and "MOTHER FUCKER!" Then spoken louder I continued with, "This may be stupid to ask at a time like this but I'm going to ask anyway. How's my skin?"

"Everything else is okay."

"Sure it is," I thought.

Once dressed, I high-tailed it out of Dr. Hale's office. Serious matters were on my mind like would this damn blood clot move toward my lungs or heart before I could get treatment. Another serious thing too, my angel Tracy was gone, she'd left WVCI and Shawna was now my guardian and she hadn't been put to the Pam test yet.

At home I called Shawna and filled her in on my situation. Within a half hour she'd contacted Dr. Sharman who arranged for me to go to Salem Hospital for a Venous Doppler test, a special ultrasound technique that evaluates blood as it flows through a blood vessel, including the body's major arteries and veins in the abdomen, arms, legs and neck. It was time to talk things over with John and fill him in about this new wrinkle in the on-going saga of my CLL clinical trial. He took the news like a pro and hustled me to the car with a fresh bottle of water for hydration. We arrived at Salem Hospital and were whisked to an ultrasound room.

The technician had me lie down, and with my paperwork already before him, commenced with the Venous Doppler. He also mentioned that Dr. Stack, my port guy, would interpret the results right away and then call Sharman. Talk about efficiency, this was trial health care at its best. As the ultrasound continued, the tech explained what I was viewing on the screen. He easily spotted the clot next to my port and said this could be causing the problem with the discoloration in my arm, but Stack would make the final determination. I was to wait, where else, but the waiting room.

Fifteen minutes later Dr. Stack appeared and had already confirmed what the technician suspected. A small blood clot was restricting blood flow to my left arm. He added that the clot was most likely caused by having a foreign object such as a port introduced into my body. I couldn't let him go without at least two questions.

"Could it have been caused by something like heavy lifting that might have dislodged my port a little bit?" And, "What do we do now?"

"In answer to your first question, it's possible, but not probable. Ports don't generally move after they've been inserted, but it could happen I suppose. And blood clots can occur in patients who don't have ports, or have never had ports," he added. Still, all I could think about was me and my damn spade.

"Regarding your second question, what you do now will be determined by Dr. Sharman and what he feels is best concerning your health history and the fact you're part of his clinical trial. I've already talked with him and he said Shawna will call you on your cell, so please stay here, don't go home just yet. Any other questions?" he asked politely.

I responded right away with, "No, thank you. You've been very helpful."

Our wait was a short one. Shawna called and reviewed all that'd transpired within the last hour or so and told me a prescription of the blood thinner, Xeralto, was already awaiting me at the Salem Hospital pharmacy. It was a 15 mg dosage, to be taken 2 times a day for 21 days. Also, I needed to watch for nose bleeds, gums bleeding and easy bruising and if these occurred, call her right away and Dr. Sharman would most likely want to alter my dosage and require more frequent labs to check on the drug's therapeutic levels. I asked if I should have my port removed, and she said she also had discussed this with Sharman already and he said not at this time because of my need for it and the fact that the Xeralto should take care of the clot by dissolving the present one, and preventing more from forming.

"And a few more things," Shawna added, "don't take aspirin or ibuprofen while on Xeralto and watch for any shortness of breath, chest pain and dizziness."

"Absolutely," I said. "Thanks, Shawna. Thanks for everything."

"No problem. I'm always here to help you." Shawna had passed my Pam test of her with flying colors.

We took the elevator to the pharmacy and picked up my prescription of Xeralto; my share of its cost was a whopping $150.00! It hadn't been lost on me that the drug was under investigation for causing severe internal bleeding, so bad in some cases that people had died from its use. I sure didn't want to be one of them, but I sure as heck didn't want a blood clot to kill me either. I turned my fears of the drug over to trust in Sharman and Shawna.

The last few days of September were pretty uneventful compared to the surprise of a blood clot that could have been fatal. I thanked again my lucky stars for a routine visit to my dermatologist, and Dr. Hale taking note of a condition well outside her area of expertise. If not for that woman and the quick response of my clinical trial team, I might have reached my expiration date.

So, the second month of my clinical trial was coming to a conclusion, and better still, my left arm was slowly but surely losing its purple streaks and returning to normal. Clearly the Xeralto was doing its intended job and doing it without any of the bad side-effects. I just hoped it would stay that way. I hoped lots of things would stay the way they were right now...low lymphocyte numbers, fewer instances of nausea and acid reflux, mouth free of painful sores, no infections to fight, the ease of a smaller 'Billie Jean Spleen' and best of all, my buddy always in the field outside my treatment room window.

I SPOOKED MYSELF IN OCTOBER

The day before I started chemo treatments for October, I got my flu shot at Salem Clinic. The waiting room was bursting with unmasked people coughing and sneezing, sending droplets as far as 5 feet and as fast as the speed limit outside. I quickly took facial protection from my purse and covered my mouth and nose, with loops placed snuggly behind my ears. I was the patient with leukemia, and I didn't want to get sick at a doctor's office while waiting for the chance to not get sick with the flu later! Sitting next to me, a blue-tinted hair senior used her walker to travel to the reception desk for a mask and quickly put hers on just in time to catch a spray of wetness that would have covered the counter. Back sitting down, she kleenexed her runny nostrils, gave me a pleasant look and then again covered her face.

I always got my flu shot early as a precaution, even though I knew with leukemia it'd never offer me the same protection afforded others without the disease. Still, I believed it was stupid NOT to be proactive and do all I could to stay healthy. If the shot only gave me 30% protection instead of a normal 60% rate, why throw out the lower number because it wasn't higher. It was still a whole lot more than zero.

Chemo on Wednesday, October 7th , started at 7:45 am and I received my usual, "Hello Pam," from the nice lady who checked me in for my initial blood work before getting approval to start treatment. Every once in a while Sharman wanted the draw from my arm rather than my friendly port and it was one of those times. I'd gotten into the habit of hydrating so well my pee was crystal clear instead of yellow tinted and my left arm was warmed to a toasty degree. And of course, those butterfly needles were always a godsend, as were experienced phlebotomists who often worked with vein-challenged patients such as I. My four vials of blood were immediately sent to the lab and in a few minutes I found out from Shawna I was a 'go' for treatment that day and tomorrow, marking my 3rd month on the clinical trial.

"Your neutrophil count is above 1.0," stated Shawna as she sat down beside John and me. "How do you feel?"

"Feeling pretty good, but a little apprehensive about taking Xeralto," I answered and then continued, "Still, my arm looks better so it's doing its job. And unless I'm imagining it, that tiny tightness by my port isn't so bad anymore either."

"Well, that's good news," she said. "And I've talked with Sharman again and he wants you to stay on the Xeralto for 21 days and then we'll get you in for a second Venous Dopplar at Salem Hospital to make sure that clot has fully dissolved."

"Will you take care of those arrangements?" asked John.

"Yes, I'll take care of everything. The appointment will be in late November; before Thanksgiving."

I breathed a sigh of relief and thanked Shawna for all her help. The three of us walked to the treatment area and, once again, sitting in the "Reserved" brown recliner, was a first timer with a look of terror on her face. I wanted to go over, wrap my arms around her and take all my feelings of hope, and empty them into her so she wouldn't be so afraid, so lost and alone. As I sat down just a chair away, I watched the drugs enter her system and watched another cancer patient hold on for dear life.

Treatment for me that day and the next went again without a glitch. I was part of a well oiled machine that'd found its groove and was heading down the final stretch. Even my Neulasta shot on Friday went great, with less sting than Monday's flu shot. And to top that off, Greer Brothers Landscaping was ready to turn our yard into a thing of beauty, and even more important, Halloween, one of my favorite times of the year, was just around the corner!

Yard work and ghost and goblins were in my future; sooooo much better than cancer, cancer, cancer.

Monday, October 13th, I felt good, even though I anticipated some nausea from my chemo a few days earlier. But I didn't even feel like I MIGHT vomit. My changed body simply felt, dare I say it, NORMAL. And with this sense of normality I turned my attention to two things... a debate between Hillary Rodham Clinton and Bernie Sanders, and the workings of the Greers.

The debate was exciting, pitting 2 seasoned public servants against one another, sharing with the viewers their vision for America after the Obama administration ended. John and I listened carefully, glad to hear about specific plans for improving health care and ways to make sure Medicare and Social Security would continue so one day Syd and Aiden's parents could benefit from what they'd paid into. Most importantly, I examined the character of each person; their honesty, abidance of the rule of law and their capacity for empathy...the ability to experience and feel what someone else is going through. I wanted some of what country lawyer Atticus Finch taught his two children in the famous novel by Harper Lee, TO KILL a MOCKINGBIRD.

With my head no near a toilet, I listened while some of the moderator's questions labeled Bernie a socialist and Hillary incompetent because of Benghazi and her emails. Both candidates were flawed in their own way, but I sensed an earnestness to move our nation forward in the world while at the same time helping those in greatest need. Having a woman hold the highest office in our country, the most powerful office on the planet, was something I'd always longed for. This longing first got a strong foothold when I was in 3rd grade and a boy at Cummings Elementary School told me I couldn't play dodge ball on his team because, "I threw like a girl." I took my rubber ball and aimed it for his head before my better self set the round thing quietly on the ground and I quickly sprinted toward the swings. Hopefully, in my grand-daughter's time a woman will sit at The Resolute Desk and if somebody "throws like a girl" it's no longer a put down, but instead, a compliment.

The next day, a Tuesday, Greer people came just after sun up and boy was I pumped. Like a kid who'd been waiting for Christmas, I greeted them and shook hands with the crew chief. We made sure we were on the same page with the job description and then they commenced tearing up the sod in the front and back yards. What would have taken me and my purple arm and big spleen weeks and weeks to accomplish, they did in a few hours. I'd picked the right workers, just like I'd picked the right CLL oncologist.

Soon the Greer crew put down sod where our backyard grass had been and in the front, removed every blade of old dying green and created two amazing dry river beds. The men were artists and my yard, their canvas.

I LOVE our Keizer beach and always will, but for years I'd longed for more. The space outside my home is not simply a yard; it's an extension of my being and a genuine source of great happiness and peace. That night I put to rest another dream of bad guy lymphocytes on a killing spree and instead thought only of fescue grass, New Zealand flax, decorative rocks, Elfin Pink step-ables and a thick layer of fresh Hemlock bark.

Early Wednesday morning John and I hastened to Al's Nursery again for more of our wants and wishes and when we got back home, I spread rolls and rolls of landscape cloth over the barren soil and both of us carefully planted our purchases. Later that afternoon, Bark Boys blew in 12 yards of dark hemlock and our front yard did an about turn from ugly to gorgeous. It was spectacular! My bark smelled better than any perfume on the market, and my igneous, sedimentary, and metamorphic rocks looked lovelier than any diamond mined deep in the bowels of the earth.

Now my attention turned toward Halloween, another great diversion from leukemia and the fight against a 3rd cancer. In celebration of the eve of All Saint's Day, and as a teacher at South High, I dressed like a witch in full costume and make-up and handed out candy to everyone who walked by my classroom. Better yet, every year I put on a party for my students. It cost me a fortune in decorations, food, drinks and 'goodie bags' but happily I footed the bill. For one day a year I let down my guard as teacher and became entertainer extraordinaire. Pumpkin carving took the place of studying literature and editing rough drafts, and downing ghostly refreshments and beverages did the trick while watching clips of classic horror films. Of course, selected parts of the frightening flicks were appropriately edited for teenage audiences; I liked my job and really wanted to keep it.

On the 28th John and I picked Aiden up from his Montessori pre-school and buckled him and his best bud, Gabriel, in their car seats and headed toward the pumpkin patch at Fordyce Farms, a few miles outside of Salem. Excitement filled our Ford as they discussed who was going to find the biggest pumpkin and climb the pyramid of baled hay the fastest. Like the happiness of all kids, what they had was contagious for us adults.

After finding a parking spot, we jumped out of the car and quickly trotted toward the hundreds of pumpkins in the big patch and then began the VERY serious work of finding the perfect specimen.

"What do you think of this, Aiden?" asked John, who'd found a bright orange one with curled stem on top.

"Bigger Grandpa, bigger!" he exclaimed.

"Okay," answered my hubby as I helped Gabrielle who was eyeing a pumpkin a few yards away. Both kids were having a ball, almost besides themselves with so many choices and row upon row of jack-o-lanterns for the making.

After the pumpkins were carefully selected and deposited in the trunk of our car, then began the fun of the corn maze and straw pyra-mid. John joined in with the boys as I watched from the sidelines, tak-ing pictures and making a mental memory of the day. Then suddenly and totally out of the blue, right smack in the middle of our wonderful day, I felt an overpowering sadness and spooked myself with the ter-rible thought of, "What if I'm not here next Halloween; what if I'm dead?" I don't know why I went there, but I did; my own worst enemy, myself, was at it again. I desperately needed to get my mind off what my mind wanted to think about. During my struggle, it was a little boy who finally came to my rescue.

He sprinted towards me, out of breath and his cheeks a bright red. "I love pumpkins, Grandma! But I love you more!" he yelled. I stood up and gave him a twirl-around hug. "Love pumpkins too Aiden," I said and then as we hugged harder added, "But I love you more!" At warp speed, I shoved thoughts of self-imposed gloom away and instead filled myself up with lots of pumpkins and one precious little boy. The ability to stop sabotaging my own happiness on a day of great joy was a huge achievement for me, HUGE. I'd struggled with it during my breast cancer and even more so with Merkel Cell Carcinoma, so pulling myself out of a Pam induced funk was really something. Maybe Aiden was my "jump start" or maybe I was learning to change my thought patterns on my own; I wasn't sure.

It was tradition, and had been for many years, that our daughter and her family put on a big Pumpkin Carving Party for friends, family and people in the neighborhood. And on October 30th, their home's four car garage magically turned into a ghost and goblin place of ping pong, air hockey and foosball, mounds of food, and long tables stocked with carving tools.

Everyone brought their own pumpkins and the frenzy to clean out the innards and commence with carving scary faces was always the highlight of the evening. Things were perfect; I was still feeling really good, except for my momentary lapse into melancholy in the pumpkin patch, and on a high after beating Karin at ping pong and only losing to John by four goals in a boisterous game of foosball. By the way, who in their right mind invented foosball; a game of tiny twirling men attached to poles that a player pulls back and pushes forward. Maybe if I ever won at foosball I'd think differently about the game's merit, but I doubt it.

A couple hours into the party the pumpkins were all carved and with candles lit inside, they looked fantastic! The best two had actually been sculpted, one a Frankenstein face and the other a very convincing,

Bela Lugosi as Dracula. Most of the kids made their pumpkins with triangle eyes and noses, and smiles with pointy teeth, but a few branched out by adding ears from the left over carvings and some even made hair from the scooped out insides. We lined up behind our creations, and Karin snapped the traditional picture for posting later on Facebook.

Halloween was the next night and the October fun continued at its best. We were at the Monekes by 5:00 o'clock, laden with our dinner for six of Love, Love Teriyaki, a quick meal before trick or treating the blocks around Summit Avenue. Aiden was costumed as an alligator and Sydney, a black cat with a long tail and white whiskers, while all us adults decided to forgo any disguises and simply be our scary selves. We were ready to head out the front door when Snow White and Superman rang the bell.

"Trick or Treat!" they yelled in unison as their parents shouted a friendly "Hello" from the drive-way, and added, "Be sure to thank everybody."

"Well, who do we have here?" asked a delighted Drew as he directed each youngster to take two pieces of candy. "Thank you very much," said the Disney personality and pint-sized DC Comics character. The cuteness was almost too much to bear as I watched the scene with two other animals close by my side.

We all spent the night chaperoning the kiddos as they raced from one house to the other filling their containers with Snickers, Red Vines, Almond Joys, and Twix Bars. The mad run for candy occurred under a clear sky of stars and quarter moon with not even a gust of wind or drop of Oregon rain.

Things couldn't have been better that 31st of October; I was with my family, I was enjoying Mother Nature and best of all, the spooky cares of CLL were fading. October definitely seemed to be my "turn around" month.

BEING THANKFUL IN NOVEMBER

I woke up the morning of November 1, 2015, thankful that I was more than half way through my chemotherapy treatments and that October had been great except for my spooking mishap. Also, Turkey Day was approaching AND we'd get our Christmas tree at the end of the month. The only thing that could up my mood even more was the chance to visit Neskowin in the near future and feed some Milkbones to my favorite resident, a golden retriever by the name of McKenzie.

We traveled the 68 miles to Springfield on Wednesday, November, 4th and arrived at 10:00 am for my blood work. My results showed: WBC, 2.3; HGB, 12.5; PLT, 120; LY#, 0.25; RBC, 4.15. Even though some of these results were lower than the reference range, the ones I wanted higher were real close to normal and the lymphocytes I wanted to keep low were staying down. And another bit of good news was my ever important ANC, better known as "absolute neutrophil count". It was holding steady at 1.6.

Pat gave me a thorough once over in the exam room and then left and another person introduced as Luisa came in. Shawna fired a series of familiar trial questions at me such as, "How was my fatigue level? Had I been experiencing any nausea? Was I bothered again by acid reflux or mouth sores? Were night sweats occurring?"

"None," I answered to all of them and wondered who this Luisa person was and why the new addition stood next to my clinical trial nurse.

"Well, you sure look good. I definitely think any of the bad side effects are in the past. But you know to call us if anything comes up, okay?" Shawna asked.

"No more waiting around," exclaimed my hubby.

"Exactly," agreed Shawna. "You definitely know the drill by now."

Then an uncomfortable quiet filled the room while Shawna straightened papers in my CLL file, and I looked at John and he looked at me and we both looked at Luisa. Finally her presence was explained and once again the handoff to a new clinical trial nurse started. From Betty, to Tracy, from Tracy to Shawna, from Shawna to Luisa; I didn't worry about anyone passing the "Pam Test" anymore. I'd learned my lesson for good. WVCI was the best place to be and Sharman and his staff were the best people to have.

Luisa, John, and I walked to the treatment area where I settled into my chair as usual. Squirrel retrieved a couple of warm blankets for me and Sarah arrived for the routine check of my blood pressure, oxygen content and temperature. I'd become quite a pro at sticking out my arm at the perfect angle, giving her the index finger on my right, not left hand and opening my mouth wide and lifting my tongue j..u..s..t s..o for the thermometer. Luisa stood by my side, watching carefully.

Premeds of .25 mg Palonosetron IV, 20 mg Dexamethasone IV, 2 tablets each of 500 mg of oral Acetaminophen, along with the hypersensitivity drugs of 50 mg Diphenhydramine IV, 100 mg Hydrocortisone IV and 125 mg Methylprednisolone IV began. As usual, they were a wonderful cornucopia of preventative measures against anything Bendamustine and Gazyva might have up their sleeve for me on any given day. Luisa left when her cell rang and she needed privacy.

Treatment followed with my clinical trial nurse returning to my side and me watching the sky over the hills off in the distance. Dark clouds were moving from the coast range and my special friend sniffed the air as her mane ruffled in the wind. With John on an errand at Starbucks, a tall mocha for himself and green tea and warmed croissant for me, I pulled my blankets up higher and read some of the many sayings on the windows that morning. "Cancer may have started the fight, but I will finish it." "Cancer, I'm going to kick your ass." "Wake up every day and battle that cancer 'til it's gone."

All these etchings had interesting messages, but more and more I was coming to the realization that our bodies often give out through no fault of our own, and certainly not from lack of trying. Those of us with cancer WANT to finish the fight; WANT to kick ass; and we really WANT to battle The Big C. But more 'want', just like the increased desire to land more left hooks and perfect more fancy footwork in the boxing ring of cancer doesn't automatically equal more success. We can be the biggest, strongest and smartest of fighters but still be overwhelmed and defeated by an opponent who doesn't care one iota about us living to see our grandkids get married some day. So maybe referring to cancer as something we can overcome by **fighting, kicking ass and battling** wasn't exactly the way to look at it.

As rain began pouring down from the rooftop and splattering the windows, I turned my eyes to a few other messages. They included their original authors. "Every day may not be good, but there's something good in every day." (Alice Morse Earle) "Cancer is only going to be a chapter in your life, not the whole story." (Joe Wasser) "Cancer is not a death sentence, but rather it is a life sentence; it pushes one to live." (Marcia Smit) "She stood in the storm and when the wind did not blow her way, she adjusted her sails." (Elizabeth Edwards) I liked these messages so much more than the others because they focused on something we could control, our ATTITUDE toward our disease. Put simply, we have the ability to use cancer for more things than cancer can use us.

"How are you feeling?" asked Luisa, my newest angel of the flock at WVCI.

"I'm doing okay. Pretty used to things now. How are you doing?" She seemed taken aback by my question about her well-being.

"Oh, I'm fine too," she said while pulling up the chair John had vacated to make his coffee run. "Know it must be an adjustment getting still another clinical trial nurse."

"Don't worry about it; I'm not, really I'm not. It was hard though when I was first starting out."

Luisa quickly followed with, "Well, let me know if any side-effects, new or old, become a problem." She handed me her card which had her cell number circled in red. "My job is to help you finish the trial and your three year follow-up." I liked the sound of that and like Humphrey Bogart said to Claude Rains in the movie, CASABLANCA, "I think this is the beginning of a beautiful friendship."

Luisa got up and went to the nurse's station to check on drugs for another patient and John returned with my drink and food, and two mochas.

"Where's Luisa?" he asked.

"Over at the station." He walked over and handed her a coffee.

As is common with clinical trials, new side-effects of the drugs being tested warrant an updating of originally signed consent forms and this is what happened in my case as part of my appointment with Sharman on Thursday, November 5th. Luisa, now well on the way to becoming my buddy with wings, directed me to page 11 of 20 of the document and this is what she read aloud:

Hole in Gut (GI Perforation)
If you have a cancer involving your gut, it is possible
That after the treatment with study drug, you may
Develop holes in your gut as the cancer cells are killed.
You may require surgery to correct this defect.
In rare cases, it may lead to death.

'Hole in the Gut' sounded so barbaric and definitely without medical euphemistic consideration. I didn't have gut problems and pitied those patients who had pre-existing ones. With all the other common, less common and rare risk factors associated with Bendamustine and Gazyva, now people had to deal with another way the trial might kill them. I wondered if some would drop out of treatment, just like I once considered doing in August, or remain to take their chances for remission from their advancing CLL.

My premeds and treatment on Thursday, after this new update and my signature on the 'Reconsent' form, went well under the supervision of Luisa. Only 191 mg of Bendamustine flowed through my veins rather than Wednesday's combo. Shawna stopped by with a quick hello just as Luisa was reminding me of my Neulasta shot the next day at Salem Hematology. It'd been a good, uneventful day free of surprises and spooks.

Back in Keizer, I settled in to watch some TV when suddenly a heartbreaking commercial about the terrible abuse of animals came on the screen. It showed dogs left out in freezing weather without shelter and shivering in the cold, horses whose bodies were no more than skin and bones and cats inside rusty cages, clearly suffering from eye infections and starving to death. They needed my help. They didn't require a well funded clinical trial to live and thrive; they just needed a willingness on my part to donate a meager $19.00 a month to the ASPCA. The poor animals needed ME to put aside my CLL woes and think outside myself, to think about their welfare for a change. Nineteen dollars wasn't enough to give either; I pledged $35.00 a month and decided to limit my Starbucks to cover the cost. That evening and many more, I invited Charlie to snooze by my side all night, bad breath and fur dander be damned.

I had my Neulasta shot at 2:00 on Friday and cringed again when I wrote o the co-pay check. Surely I would have no trouble hitting my out of pocket maximum for 2015.

The weekend was wonderful, with a visit from the grandkids and their parents on Saturday afternoon. I mentioned the ASPCA to them and how good it felt to help animals like the ones I'd seen on TV. The kiddos right away wanted to help too. Their pets, Wilson, Boots, and Rainman all had been adopted from the local humane society so that seemed to be the perfect place to target our energy, doing something for the animals in our own community. Suddenly an idea emerged, we'd put on a Summer Art Fair and sell things we knew how to make, like rainbow loop bracelets and necklaces, cards and stationery, potholders, scarves, artwork, and lots more. The great thing was we already had mounds and mounds of them done, and with it only being November, we had months to make more crafts and think up new ones. All the money and donations, every penny of it, we'd give to the Willamette

Valley Humane Society. The best part of the whole idea was no longer were we just taking the easy way and TALKING about helping animals, we had a plan and were going to put it into ACTION. We discussed our Summit Fair for a long time that afternoon and I was still riding high when my head hit the pillow that night.

What goes up must come down and the next morning I awoke with a runny nose, sinus pressure, nasty cough, and temperature of 99.6%. I hydrated and began a Tylenol regiment of 500 mg. every four hours, hoping I'd miraculously be well in 24 hours, but I should have known better.

I made a frantic call to Dr. Sharman's office on Tuesday November 10th and Luisa got me in right away. He confirmed a low grade fever and did blood work which showed a seriously diminished platelet count. He attributed it to the BG treatment and told me not to worry. When the neutrophil results finally popped up on his computer, he looked relieved to see them still holding strong, even though I'd definitely picked up a bug that was worsening, fast.

"How can I feel so good Saturday and Sunday and feel so lousy today?" I asked Sharman.

"We're going to start you on Azithromycin and it'll get you better quickly. Having CLL and going through a clinical trial certainly makes you more vulnerable to infections than other people, but remember, healthy people get sick too, especially at this time of year. You didn't do anything wrong, Pam."

John smiled at me and said, "It'll be okay, Rabbit," which made me feel a little better.

"And I'm taking you off Xeralto," Dr. Sharman added. "We had you on a higher dosage for the first 21 days to make sure that clot didn't move on us and then a lower dosage to dissolve it for sure. It's now been 48 days and there's every indication the problem no longer exists. For peace of mind though, I'll have Luisa schedule another Veinous Dopplar for you at Salem Hospital before Thanksgiving so it won't interfere with any turkey day plans. How's that?"

"That's great," I exclaimed. Knowing I hadn't done anything wrong to bring on my infection and that antibiotics would "kick its ass," I was already feeling better. And if my second Dopplar turned out normal, well I'd be on top of the world. Luisa returned with my prescription and carefully went over the instructions with John and me. Then she explained, "I'll call the hospital in Salem this afternoon and make the Dopplar arrangements. Is it okay if I email you when everything's finalized?"

"Sure," I replied, knowing full well she'd do exactly what she said she'd do.

That whole week I worked to get myself healthy again. I downed at least a half gallon of Smart Water daily, checked my temperature every four hours to make sure it wasn't hitting 100.4%, got plenty of rest and above all else, took my prescribed medication. Also during that time, Luisa called to schedule a follow-up appointment for 12:30 pm on Monday the 17th , as well as another Veinous Dopplar for Monday, the 23rd. I forced myself not to dwell on something my little pee brain had sent out invitations for; thoughts of what life would be like someday without Sharman and Luisa always having my back.

By the weekend, I was completely recovered so I drove to the Courthouse Tennis Center and cheered on my buddies who won in a tie breaker against a strong group of Eugene players. I was thrilled to see everyone! For our reunion I'd gussied up myself with eye shadow and Maybelline mascara, Cover Girl lipstick, recently cut and colored hair, and a new pair of Levi's, which by the way, were a size smaller than before entering into a relationship with Bendamustine and Gazyva. A pretty top from Chico's completed my make-over and I was having thoughts about playing competitive tennis again. It's amazing how improving one's appearance on the outside can improve one's confidence on the inside.

On the 16th, a Monday, I had blood drawn to test for Merkel oncoprotein antibodies; if my numbers left the negative range and went up above 74, then I was in trouble. The heck with worrying about CLL, a recurrence of Merkel carcinoma was by far the greater concern because its rarity and aggressiveness had fewer treatment options and much swifter rate of death. The two to three week wait for test results from Seattle was excruciating.

When Sharman checked me out on the 17th he gave me a clean bill of health, for the sinus infection anyway, and supplied me with the good news that my platelet count was now back up in the normal range. Hip, hip, horray! He also wrote me another prescription of Azithromycin to have on hand, reminding me once again of the importance of catching things as early as possible.

Syd's music program was on Thursday, the 19th at Walker Middle School where I'd attended junior high. Talk about a trip down memory lane. My time there marked me having my first serious boyfriend, a cute and kind-hearted soul by the name of Kenny, and us locking hands in the darkened cafeteria after lunch while CREATURE FROM THE BLACK LAGOON scared the younger 7th and 8th graders around us.

As I sat in the gym waiting for Sydney's class to perform, I gazed up at the rings hanging a little ways down from the ceiling and remembered myself swinging across from bleacher to bleacher like a baby monkey who felt no fear of falling. Never once in gym class at Walker did I ever worry about my health, except maybe getting my period and being horrified if a drop of red showed through the crotch of my white PE shorts. Now I was an old woman with an old body who'd had breast cancer, Merkel, and now CLL. Before further melancholy set in, I turned my attention to the wonder of my grand-daughter as she sang with her class and then played a piano solo of "Ode to Joy" by the very famous, Ludwig van Beethoven.

After I'd ventured out of the house on Thursday evening for something more than a doctor's appointment or shot of Neulasta, I was on a roll and excited about the coffee "date" my hubby and I had planned for Friday. We bundled up early that morning in our Neskowin, flannelled-lined jackets with hoods and walked to Starbucks on River Road, about half a mile away. After ordering two coffees and a cranberry/orange scone, we scouted the place for some overstuffed chairs and considered ourselves lucky when a couple left and we got to the furniture before anyone else. We settled in nicely.

"So, how you doing, Rabbit?" asked John while sipping his seasonal chestnut praline.

"I don't want to jinx things, but I'm feeling pretty good."

"What do you mean "jinx" things?"

"Well, you know it seems like whenever I think I've turned the corner on cancer, the damn thing sneaks up from behind and grabs me in a strangle-hold again and I'm hanging on for dear life. It REALLY gets old after awhile, you know?"

"I know; I've been there with you," he softly replied. "And I wouldn't have it any other way." He paused slightly and then added, "Pinky swear."

Saturday and Sunday I went on an energized terror, decorating our home for Christmas. Stockings for us and the grandkids took their usual place hanging from the mantle in the living room, and Frosty the Snowman, in all his different sizes and shapes, were placed in every conceivable location. Two giant Mr. and Mrs. Claus held chocolate tipped candy canes next to the front door and artificial wreaths adorned every room, both downstairs and up. My two favorite decorations, a little string of gingerbread people and an old wooden sign painted red with Santa and his sleigh pulled by reindeer took their places where our family would see them most often. The gingerbread youngsters were above the kitchen window and next to our big TV in the family room, the sign with its picture of St. Nick and message of, "I Believe in Santa Claus." Hardly a wall or piece of furniture was without a touch of Christmas spirit. I took it all in and my heart smiled. I was a child again living in my old Keizer homes on Manbrin Drive and Birch Avenue, snug and safe, unafraid of cancer and its ability to whisk me away from those I love.

On Monday, November 23rd, I balanced the day with my second Dopplar at Salem Hospital in the morning and the kiddos with us in the afternoon. The first event was a "had to" and the second, a "want to."

The technician went through her instructions and even though the procedure was painless, watching the screen's televised findings was nerve racking. John, the lady and me all breathed a big sigh of relief when the test showed no indication of the blood clot that'd been diagnosed just two months earlier. The Xeralto had been successful and I could now quit worrying so much about that setback interfering with the rest of my CLL clinical trial.

Sydney and Aiden burst through our front door later in the day, and with them brought all the love any grandparent could ever hope for. One moment our home felt so empty and the next minute every square foot of every room was full of their little kid presence. As I got on my knees to say "Hello" at their level, Sydney wrapped her arms around my neck and hung on tightly. Aiden snuck beside her and leaned forward with a wet kiss to my cheek.

"How are the best grandkids in the world?" I asked, the compliment always repeated every time we came together.

Syd answered first with, "I'm doing great, Grandma!"

"Me too!" chimed in her little brother, quick to follow his big sister's lead.

"WONDERFUL!" I exclaimed as they peeled off me and greeted Grandpa with the exact same enthusiasm.

Karin showed me the bag with the things they'd brought for their visit, necessities like Aiden's tiny blue blanket and Syd's well worn green one, special stuffed animals, and a few toys. "Is it okay if I pick them up in a few hours, say around 5:00 o'clock so we can have dinner at home together?"

"Sure. That sounds fine," I responded. "Thanks for bringing them." Karin scooted out the door to get her weekly shopping done at Costco and try to squeeze in a little housecleaning for Thanksgiving Day. I remembered all too well the years I hosted Thanksgiving dinner for our families and everything that went into it. The hosting tradition had been passed on to our daughter years ago and although she handled the task with skill and grace, it also burdened her. I could see it in her eyes.

"Well, what do you guys want to do first?" I asked the two excited, little kids standing in front of me. That simple question started the first of our 10 games of hide and seek, doing crafts for our art fair, Ninja warrior sword fighting, card games of Exploding Kittens, and a long Monopoly contest. The time sped by quickly, with an occasional break to watch KC Undercover and have a healthy snack plate. Of course Grandpa added a couple of chocolate covered almonds on the side and handed them a cup of chocolate milk before I could pour their 2 % regular Darigold. They giggled when they saw me being over-ruled and they knew very well neither of us liked contradicting the other. "And really, what harm could a little bit of sugar do?" I asked myself, feeling not the least bit tired from our long play date. I was definitely getting stronger and stronger; I could feel it.

Thanksgiving came and went quickly, but with a lasting memory of both sides of the family all gathered around a beautifully set table, Syd's little cards telling us where to sit, and a bouquet of flowers placed center stage. We used Karin's best dishes to eat from, and lovely cloth napkins to wipe our mouths with, and everyone waited until all were finished eating before leaving the table. It reminded me of the meals at my grandparents' homes, before the age of TV trays and everyone going their separate ways to chow down. It was civilized and genteel and polite; it was very nice.

On Friday the 27th, we all met at Palmers' Christmas Tree Farm on Poinsettia Lane. We'd been going for years because the selections were great and the kiddos got free hot chocolate and candy canes. Also, the prices were reasonable and Palmers shook the trees after cutting and then baled them tightly so they could fit easily into any size vehicle. Walking through the acres and acres of Christmas trees, John finally picked out our five foot noble and Drew supervised the selection of their 10 foot grand fir, each tried and true Oregon natives in terms of lasting power and limb strength; both the guys and the trees. The husbands cut the trees down using hand saws as us women folk and Aiden cheered them on from a safe distance.

Once home, John carried in our noble, placed it in a heavy metal stand, cut the baling string and got the tree perfectly turned so the best side stood forward. After putting water in the container as my hubby went upstairs, I started decorating the evergreen with its string of lights first and ornaments second. I was in my 'happy place', home, surrounded by my Santas and Frosties, the smell of tree needles, and Bing Crosby's

'I'm Dreaming of a White Christmas' floating through the air.

Then POW! I was hit with the same thing that had happened in October, the gut-wrenching fear that I wouldn't be around next year. Instead of joining in the fun of Christmas and being by my family's side, I'd be ashes inside our pretty starfish urn, courtesy of Keizer Funeral Parlor on River Road, N.

Maybe everyone would share stories about past Christmases, but I wouldn't be there to laugh with them, hug and kiss them; help them survive in a world full of scary and bad things. I'd be NOWHERE. I'd done it again, torpedoed my own state of happiness and bombed into rubble, my peaceful, quiet mind.

Not having Aiden and a pumpkin patch to help me, I turned the TV on to IT'S A WONDERFUL LIFE, picked some needles from a limb and rubbed them between my fingers so Christmas smelled up close and personal. I then sat down on the couch to read some things. Ever since 1991, I'd written summaries of the previous years and kept all the pages tied together and placed in a special Xmas box. Instead of journal entries that picked out daily events, these pages summed up the important occurrences during a twelve month's span. Looking back over time instead of worrying about the future, they helped me realize the good in life far outweighed the bad. Problems that once seemed insurmountable had been overcome and life's painful episodes had passed. Time didn't heal all wounds, but it helped make the bleeding stop. I finished reading my last summary, dated 2014, and watched Jimmy Stewart run through the snow of Bedford Falls, elated and with a new appreciation of a life worth so much more than the payout of a life insurance policy.

Over the weekend I rested up for my final days of Bendamustine, Gazyva and Neulasta. Similar to August, December had multiple treatment days, 4 to be exact, with 2, rather than 1, Neulasta shots in the mix. Unlike any holiday season I'd ever experienced before though, I wanted it done and over and as fast as possible.

A HOLLY JOLLY DECEMBER

December 1ˢᵗ fell on a Tuesday, a day I teemed with energy. I attacked Amazon's site for a few more Christmas presents, visited Safeway for weekly groceries, changed the beds, scrubbed toilets and sinks, washed floors and with a vengeance, dusted and vacuumed our old carpet. I REALLY wanted to get my house and life in order for the last month of the clinical trial and ready myself for the new beginning of a much lower lymphocyte count and smaller spleen. Squirrel, knowing me as he does, stayed out of my cross-hairs and let me go at whatever hectic pace I craved. I always knew I'd married a very smart man.

We arrived for chemo treatment number 13 at 10:00 am on Wednesday morning. My blood draw was again by way of my port, which I still eyed with some suspicion ever since the clot episode. Most of my numbers remained stable, but one, however, worried Dr. Sharman and that meant I was worried too. My platelets were now a low 107, a drop of 13 since a month ago. WBC was on the rise as it moved a bit closer to normal and neutrophils were holding steady, but my CLL specialist didn't look too happy about my blood clotting ability. He told Luisa to schedule an appointment for the 16th. Clearly, he didn't want to wait until the last week in December for my final two treatments to check on those platelets.

"Yep, never a dull moment with cancer," I thought to myself and quickly added another insight to my already addled chemo brain.

"Time outs hardly ever happen when competing against the Big C."

I found my favorite recliner unoccupied so sat my ass down and settled in for good viewing of my sweet, dependable horse, and clear sight lines across the parking lot to the familiar hills north of town. With the cold weather of December, the warm blankets felt better than ever and when John took my order for a Starbuck's iced coffee, I changed it to a steaming hot peppermint mocha.

Katy accessed my port, did the premeds, and soon the chemo drugs surged through my veins like old friends traveling on vacation together. I marveled again at how something so foreign and frightening a few months ago had now become so commonplace. The morning cruised by with Gazyva and Bendamustine going into me. Thursday came and went with just Benda, and then the Neulasta shot on Friday, the 4th.

No terrible side-effects plagued my body as they once did, and I was closer than ever to being my old self when I took Syd to have tea with Mrs. Claus on the 13th. We're not 'foo-foo' females so we wore our nice jeans and Old Navy tops while most others in attendance were attired in frilly dresses and fancy hats. My grand-daughter and I are firm believers that comfort trumps ruffles in the same way 'Love trumps Hate.'

We lunched on small, triangular-shaped cucumber and cream cheese sandwiches and sweet chutney filled scones while sipping Japanese cherry blossom tea from dainty cups. Mrs. Claus talked about her husband and all the elves who worked so hard to make good little boys and girls happy on Christmas Day. Syd was at that age when belief in Santa and the whole sled of flying reindeer thing teetered back and forth between truth and falsehood, but that afternoon for my sake I watched her lean toward the unbelievable. She knew her believing would bring me joy, so as Mrs. Claus continued her magical stories during dessert and hot chocolate, Syd played along with lots of 'oohs' and 'aahs'.

On Monday, December 14th, I spent almost two hours waiting in the lobby of Salem Clinic for my usual blood draw for Merkel. The last time had been in September and here I was again. I'd hydrated to beat the band that morning, three full bottles of Smart Water, and tried to keep my left arm warm with a newly microwaved hot pack, but it'd turned cold after the first hour. I requested my favorite phlebotomist to improve my chances of getting a good poke the first time and patiently waited my turn by playing solitaire on my cell.

Like last time at the clinic, a few nearby patients coughed and blew their noses so I put on my mask and cleaned my hands with one of the many tiny SANI-HANDS wipes I kept in my purse. Finally I was called back to the lab, but not by Keri.

"Where's Keri?" I asked the man in the starched white lab coat as he led the way.

"She's taking a few days off," he stated abruptly. "Sit down and let's get you taken care of," he added. His voice sounded like the starched coat he wore, sterile and harsh.

"You'll need to warm my left arm and use a butterfly needle," I pleasantly informed him. "My veins aren't in the best shape and the real good one has quite a bit of scar tissue around it." I smiled, expecting his easy compliance.

"I don't think that'll be necessary," he stated with authority as he readied a big needle and alcohol swab. He acted like he knew me better than I knew myself and my veins.

I'm NOT a complainer, and I always try to be nice to people, especially those in charge of my medical care and certainly those who stand in front of me with big needles. But this guy was wrong, dead wrong. As he vigorously tapped my left arm searching for a vein and finding none, I decided to take matters into my own hands and said for all to hear in the lab, "I want another phlebotomist."

He glared at me and removed the band he'd tied around my upper arm and then slowly backed away from my chair. I'd done the last thing I ever wanted to do, draw attention to myself in public, but I figured it was a darn good time. I didn't need a half dozen pokes and a badly bruised arm to ruin my holidays.

"What's the matter over here?" questioned a lab supervisor who came to my rescue.

"I want my arm warmed and a butterfly needle used," I said flatly.

"This gentleman doesn't appear to want to do that for me."

Mr. Starch Man responded with, "I didn't think there was a need for those things and besides, we're so busy this morning we're already way backed up. I'm just trying to go as fast as I can. Sorry." The starchiness in his voice had wrinkled, slightly.

"I understand," the supervisor said. "But we always do whatever we can to accommodate a patient's requests, even if we're busy. Let me handle this draw and you go on break. You haven't had one since you got here at 7:00 am and you're long overdue."

He stepped further away from my chair and repeated his "Sorry" another time before heading to the door marked, 'RESTROOM'. Part of me wanted to apologize for my behavior, as if I'd done something wrong, but the other part, the larger part of me, was proud that I'd spoken up on my own behalf. My blood was drawn with a warmed arm and butterfly needle as requested; it was a good, first try poke.

Wednesday the 16th came and John and I drove again to Dr. Sharman's office, this time to see if my low platelet count had turned the corner and was finally on the rise. Blood was taken again from my tired left arm so the most accurate reading could be achieved. In no time the good doctor came into the room, clicked on the computer and told me the bad news that my platelet numbers had gone even lower. They were now 99.

"This number is not critically low," said Sharman, "but I was hoping your platelets would be higher at this stage of your treatment."

"What if they just keep going lower?" I asked him in a worried tone of voice.

"My advice is for us not to get ahead of ourselves. It's not that uncommon for low platelet counts during treatment. I wouldn't at all be surprised if we see an increase at your next appointment on the 28th."

We looked intently at one another; patient to doctor, and both decided it was best not to travel down the road of 'what if's.' I'd done it too often before with CLL and my other cancers and the scenery wasn't pretty. We returned home to Keizer around noon and I worked to put the whole platelet dilemma aside for the time being. Worrying on the

27th would be plenty of time to address the number 99.

The eight days leading up to Christmas were pretty darn good and during that time I watched favorite re-runs of THE OFFICE and finished reading SHROUDS of GLORY...From Atlanta to Nashville: The Last Great Campaign of the Civil War by Winston Groom and THE LAST LECTURE by Randy Pausch, whose advice for all of us is, "We cannot change the cards we are dealt, just how we play the hand." Every day I also walked two miles, enjoying the cold weather and my state's fresh air. Those walks, every one of them, got my heart pounding and helped me get stronger. Cancer of the blood was becoming more and more a shadowy figure whose face was fading away.

On Christmas Eve John and I stayed home while the Monekes celebrated with Drew's side of the family. It always saddened us a bit, not to be with them, but the trade off was having them on December 25th AND having a sleep-over for the grandkids. So in the long run, I'd say we got the best part of the bargain.

The next day Karin, Drew and the kiddos arrived at 11:00 am, Syd and Aiden running through the front door first and their mommy and daddy lagging behind. After waiting patiently for the 'okay' from the adults, the kiddos took their stockings down and began opening the presents inside.

"This is exactly what I wanted!" Syd squealed as she held up a tiny sloth stuffed animal and Aiden voiced the same when he unwrapped a small OSU Beaver. Packages of Juicy Fruit Gum, fidget spinners, glow in the dark stickers, and plastic Rudolfs that pooped M & M's completed their haul.

"Wind it up again, Grandma!" Aiden yelled, having his 5th candy fall out of the red-nosed reindeer's tooshie.

"Mine too!" screamed Sydney. "Mine too!" Grandpa.

Then their mom intervened with, "That's enough sugar for now; lunch will be ready soon, won't it?" She looked at me for a 'yes' and I gave her one right away. While John snapped a couple pictures of Rudolf and the grandkids, I put out, buffet style, the guacamole dip, tacos, mac and cheese, veggies and fruit platters. We ate well and voted to postpone dessert until later. It was time to open the gifts crowded under our tree.

The frenzy of rushing through gift opening had been stopped by decree of me, the previous year. No more of this tossing presents to everyone and then everybody ripping through the wrapping paper all at the same time, devouring their long awaited surprises like wild animals eating their kills. So Sydney slowly passed out gifts, ONE at a time and each person savored the untying of ribbons and peeling off of scotch tape as we all watched. "Thank you" and "you're welcome" and hugs from receiver to giver were unrushed and every present shown great appreciation.

By 6:00 pm Karin and Drew were ready to call it a night, while the grandkids were getting their second wind. Syd and Aiden pleaded for another rousing game of 'sardines,' the ever popular variation of hide and seek, but one look at our daughter and son-in-law and I knew they needed to head home. And besides, it was time for us to officially commence our December 25th sleep-over.

"You sure you **really** want to do this Mom?" Karin asked with daughterly concern. "The kids would certainly understand. After all, you're still doing chemo and...."

"Absolutely," I answered right away. "Now you and Drew get out of here so we can play more sardines and you guys can get some rest." They left, both laden with presents, left-over food, and plenty of dessert.

The rest of the evening was all fun and games at Grandma and Grandpa's, that is until 9:00 o'clock when both kiddos dozed off on my big bed as Squirrel rubbed their backs and each snuggled with their new stuffed animals. Their soft breathing was music to my ears and all doubts about my future health never entered even a small corner of my quiet mind.

Chemo started at 9:15 am on December 28th, but as usual I had blood drawn a few minutes prior. My best Christmas present, delivered a few days late, was a higher platelet count, just like Sharman had predicted. It hadn't increased a lot at 102, but the trend was definitely upward.

While waiting for my premeds, I filled out the questionnaire Luisa had handed me and was delighted to circle 'Not at All' to the following questions:

"Were you short of breath?"

"Have you felt nauseated?"

"Have you vomited?"

"Do you have any trouble taking a long walk?"

"Does pain interfere with your daily activities?"

"Has your temperature been going up and down?"

"Have you had trouble with infections?"

Sarah did her job of checking things before my infusion nurse sprayed the skin covering my port and inserted a needle for the premeds. John brought me warm blankets, I downed some water and reclined in my comfortable chair. Searching the pasture for my old buddy, I found her just as she was unloading a big one onto the ground beneath her tail; it was nothing like Rudolf and his M & M's.

A sweet volunteer came over to show me the pretty bracelets she'd made for us cancer patients; they were tiny colored beads on a stretch band and each had a small angel near the tie. She offered me three, since she knew about Syd and Aiden, but I graciously turned her down. I didn't want my grandkids to have another reminder of my cancer because it'd filled their young lives enough already. Chemo went fine, again just like clock-work.

My final treatment, on December 29th, was just Benda. As I watched its last drip into my port I thought about all the bags and bags full of drugs that had travelled into my body over the past months, some designed to ease side effects and others to kill bad blood cells. My CLL was the 5th kind of cancer my body produced; first came breast cancer, then Merkel cell carcinoma, followed by basal and squamous skin cancers and lastly (I was going to say 'finally' but that would be wishful thinking), Chronic Lymphocytic Leukemia.

Today was a graduation of sorts; a getting through the trials and tribulations of something I'd never experienced even with all my experience with cancer, and that was chemotherapy. I felt proud that I'd made it, but frightened too, because I'd come to the end of my front line defense against a disease that would return in its attempt to take me out. As much as the combination of Gazyva and Bendamustine had done a number on me, they also improved my chances at living long enough for my grandchildren to remember me, REALLY remember me.

Before leaving, Luisa came to my side and told me a Neulasta shot was scheduled for 4:15 tomorrow afternoon. She also said Sharman wanted to do another round of blood work and have a quick visit with him on January 7th and that January 11th, would be my appointment at Salem Hospital for my port removal.

Then she added, "You'll be starting your post clinical trial tests with a CT scan, EKG and bone marrow aspiration to follow thereafter; most likely in February and March sometime. Remember, we'll be seeing you every three months for three years." She paused and added one more thing, "I'll be with you every step of the way."

"So much for a vacation from doctor visits," I kidded.

We said our 'good-byes' and hugged. Getting on my coat I glanced outside to bid farewell to my quiet, dependable companion. When no one was at my side, when I sat alone with just the drugs and the sounds and smells of everyone's fight against cancer, she roamed her field and helped calm my fears. I clung to her, with the distance between us never an impediment to my love for her. I regretted not stopping to really say "Hello," to call her over for a pet, or feed her an apple or carrot. They were lost opportunities and I didn't want my life to have anymore of them.

Writing on the window before leaving , I carefully printed the following message after I retrieved Syd and Aiden's pictures off the window sill.

We do this not just for ourselves,
but so we can live for the ones we love.

P.J.

2015

John took my hand and walked me out of the treatment room as more patients walked in. It was a continuous cycle of starting and finishing; a never ending attempt to finally coffin cancer cells once and for all. I was part of that attempt. Heading home to Keizer a light snow began to hit our windshield and in the distance, the familiar hills were already dusted in white.

MILEPOST 2016

The year 2016, started out great. On January 4th, my Merkel blood samples which had traveled to the University of Washington Medical Center, came back negative for the Merkel oncoprotein. I was elated because the result suggested my Merkel Cell Carcinoma (MCC) remained in remission. And three days later I was in Dr. Sharman's office where I was told my lymph nodes and spleen were fine and WBC, platelets lymphocytes and neutrophils were all good. "No need to worry about a thing," is the way Sharman put it.

Instead of my CBC lab reports showing lots of L's and H's outside the standard range, my blood was looking closer and closer to normal. As a result, I was riding high when my port was removed on the 11th. The anesthesiologist must have given me plenty of drugs because after a line was put in my left arm, I was in a quiet sleep until I woke back up in my room with my sweet husband asking me a very familiar question.

"How do you feel?"

My answer, "Terrific!" The ride back home was pretty darn good too because for the first time in 22 weeks, my body no longer harbored something which was not a natural part of me.

That weekend the grandkids paid us a visit and we took them swimming at the Courthouse, something they could never get enough of. To their surprise I took a big leap into the deep end instead of tip-toeing down the stairs into the shallow.

"Grandma, be careful!" shouted Syd once I'd surfaced.

"No worries," I answered. I'm much better and Billie Jean is a lot smaller." She giggled and swam over to me, and as always, her little brother shadowed her, bobbing up and down behind her kicks.

"Does that mean you can REALLY play with us like you used to?" asked Aiden.

"You betcha it does!" I yelled, wrapping them together in a single, wet hug that John joined in too.

Almost 2 hours later, we had 'prune' hands and feet and decided it was past time to get ourselves on dry land. I took Syd into the ladies' restroom and John corralled Aiden to take him to the men's. My grand-daughter and I shed our suits, put them in the spinner and prepared ourselves for a nice warm shower in stall # 1, our favorite because of its big seat and detachable nozzle.

"Can I see where your port was, Grandma?" Syd's voice sounded worried.

"Sure you can," I said.

Bending to her little girl height, I pointed to the scar where my port had been inserted, resided for treatment and then been removed.

"It looks real good," she whispered as if some female might be listening in stall #2.

"Thanks," I whispered back.

Syd had grown accustomed to my mastectomy scars, which she'd seen often and knew a little of the story behind my breast cancer. She'd also viewed me at my worst with ugly stitches covering the left side of my face, down my neck and behind my ear from Merkel surgery. I considered her a seasoned observer of my body's encounter with cancer and whenever she felt like talking about Grandma's "marks" we would.

Later that night after we returned the kiddos home, I decided it was about time to send out what would be my final email and let people know, not how the clinical trial was going, but how it had gone.

Hello Family and Friends. Thank you all VERY much for
your prayers, emails, cards, letters and phone calls as John and
I have gone through the leukemia clinical trial at Willamette

Valley Cancer Institute and Research Center in Springfield, OR.

You have helped and encouraged us every step of the way and we are forever grateful. I completed the last of my 15 treatments recently and had my port removed a few days ago at Salem Hospital. I'm feeling good and future tests/procedures later this month and during February will determine the real success of my trial.

These 6 months have been an interesting and certainly challenging experience, but my doctors and nurses did all they could to help me stay confident and hopeful. At my worst when I questioned whether or not I'd continue with treatments, I thought of all the others who'd gone through it before me and were my heroes; Debbie Faber, Char Andrews, Martina Mangan, Debbie Arnold, Brett Hall, my sweet cousin Sara, and so very many more. With them traveling that road first, I had the courage to go second. Hugs to you all and enjoy each day.

Much love, Pam

On January 25th, I had my lab work and filled out my usual questionnaire prior to seeing Dr. Sharman. Again, my blood results were good and my examination didn't find anything unusual. The healing of my port extraction had gone well so I asked Sharman about returning to tennis.

"I think that's a great idea!" he said enthusiastically. "Your spleen is only mildly enlarged and that's because of the stretching it endured holding all the cancerous lymphocytes prior to your treatment. If you feel you're up to tennis, then you should get back on the courts."

"Boy, I was hoping you'd say that. I've really missed it."

"My advice is to just take it a little easy and listen to your body. When you get tired, REST, and don't push things. And REALLY hydrate. Okay?"

"Okay," I came back as John gave me a high five. And then I added, "Maybe Johnson and Johnson can play doubles together."

"Let's not go that far right now, Rabbit. Let's get you hitting a ball a few times a week and then see what happens."

"Gotcha," I answered.

Luisa took us to a private room in the treatment area and I had my post trial EKG to check for any heart irregularities that might have developed during my months of chemotherapy. It was completely normal. Things were moving along nicely and my next visit to WVCI was scheduled for February 23rd to include my usual labs, exam by Sharman and another CT scan I'd agreed to in my consent form. January had been free of unwelcomed surprises and spooks, and I thanked my lucky stars.

February's scan was good, with no adverse reactions from the dye that was injected to highlight specific internal areas. With the second scan finished, Sharman could now compare it to my earlier one in August and determine the effectiveness of the Bendamustine/Gazyva CLL clinical trial for ME. The CT radiologist said the doctor would be notified of the results in a few days and I hoped those results would be in my favor.

Part of my birthday celebration on the 28th was playing a little tennis again. My forehand returned easily, but my backhand was pathetic, worse than the last time we'd hit at Bush Park. For the life of me I couldn't figure out why, either. I'd played the ad side for years as John's doubles' partner; the left side was "home" to me, like Keizer and Neskowin.

"Don't get frustrated, Rabbit," John sympathized. "You'll get it back. Remember after your breast surgery how long it took?"

I pouted and replied, "Yea, but I'm feeling really good now and didn't just have two tits cut off."

"Tell you what. How 'bout you take a few serves?" Just like a great teacher, he changed the task when his student got discouraged.

"Okay," I answered. My serves weren't top notch, but after he helped me with my toss and stance, they got a whole lot better. We played a few games and when he gave me two "Mulligans" I won a game, narrowly. The best part though; I didn't get tired from our play date and didn't feel any side-effects from my 6 months of treatment.

March rolled around and a lot was happening in my life. I met my special CLL Buddy Brett for coffee where we discussed latest treatments and ways to raise funds for the Leukemia and Lymphoma Society, we found a house to rent in Neskowin during the summer for our beach family vacation, I resumed playing tennis with my partner Donna and saw Dr. Sharman on the 29th for another bone marrow aspiration. I knew exactly what to expect but that didn't make the idea of large needles going into my back any less worrisome.

My post clinical trial bone marrow aspiration occurred early the morning of March 29, 2016, eight months after my first one and three months after BG chemotherapy concluded. As usual I had my routine blood work prior to seeing Dr. Sharman and Luisa and things were normal, except my neutrophil count was 0.44, at critical value, and flagged as "LL." This indicated my infection fighting capabilities were seriously low and I mean, seriously. And even though other things like platelet and lymphocyte numbers were good, I was scared. During treatment my Neulasta shots had brought my neutrophil counts up, however now they were dangerously low.

"Such a neutrophil count isn't uncommon after treatment," said Dr. Sharman as he tried to allay my fears. "We'll give it another month or so and if the numbers fail to come up, we can do something to improve them. For right now, let's allow your body to adjust and make them on its own."

John asked if it was safe to do the bone marrow aspiration for fear of infection and Sharman assured him it was. Then my hubby bid me good-bye to wait in reception while the good doctor and my wonderful clinical trial nurse steered me down the familiar hall way.

Already in the room were two assistants donned in white aprons and wearing surgical gloves readying the instruments and slides for the marrow specimens. Placed on a small metal pan were a few syringes with long needles attached. Some of them already had fluid inside; others were empty. The air smelled like it did last time, antiseptic.

"Please lay face down on the table just like before, Pam," said one of the familiar looking assistants. My heart started pounding just thinking about what was to come. I figured I was lucky with my first bone marrow aspiration and there was no way in the world that it'd go so smoothly again. Dr. Sharman was good, but was he that good? Once again I found the "enemy" in the room and it was none other than little old me.

I tried hard to comfort myself on the padded table with arms bent at the elbow, my hands tucked under my chin. Someone lifted up my blouse just a little and moved my Capri's down a tad and then placed a sterile sheet with a large opening over my lower back area. Luisa sat herself down next to me and smiled, offering words of encouragement. Sharman put on his gloves and I readied myself for what was coming. "First a little bit of lidocaine under the skin to help you feel more comfortable during the procedure," said my doctor.

"Just try to relax as much as you can, Pam," said Luisa. She rubbed my shoulders like Betty had done before, but instead of taking her advice to relax, my mind went forward from the painless prick of lidocaine to the dull pain of the first marrow test.

"I'm going to go slowly and I'll tell you everything I'm going to do before I do it. I promise," stated Sharman.

"Thanks," I answered and then added, "Don't know why I'm so jittery this time around. Maybe it's because I know better what's happening or because the results of this test are so important."

"You're doing great, Pam," Sharman encouraged. "Let's get a good sample and get you some good news." As Luisa's massage continued, I finally relaxed enough to travel from my present circumstances to Johnson's Beach in our backyard. His needle went in deeper and deeper and I breathed at a snail's pace.

"Now I'm going to remove some of the marrow fluid and we'll send it to the lab. Just a little longer, okay?" I noticed Luisa had stopped rubbing.

"Okay," I replied. "Tell me when to take a deep breath and count to 5."

"Let's do that, NOW."

I breathed in hard and Luisa and I counted slowly together... "1, 2, 3, 4, 5." The needle with its syringe came back out and was quickly given to the technicians who placed the specimens under glass slides.

"How do we look over there?" asked Sharman, checking to make sure enough marrow fluid had been removed again for testing.

"We have plenty," was the answer.

My entire body gave in to a giant, single sigh of relief. The bone marrow aspiration was over and with it one heck of a poke.

"Like before, rest for at least 20 minutes on your back to control any bleeding and your blood pressure is stable and then you're cleared to go home. How does that sound?"

"Amazing," I told my doctor.

Luisa stayed with me for the first few minutes and we talked about my neutrophil count being so low. She explained that some patients give themselves shots of Neupogen, a drug that stimulates the production of neutrophils in a person's bone marrow. She encouraged me to do some research and added that she'd email me information about neutropenic precautions, as well as arrange for Salem Clinic to do a CBC to check my neutrophils in three to four weeks. Neupogen was an option, not a necessity at this point so like Neulasta, would NOT be completely covered by the clinical trial. Bummer, again.

No bleeding occurred from my swift and skillfully executed bone marrow aspiration and my blood pressure remained at a steady 120/70 so John and I returned home to Keizer around 11:00. Mission accomplished. The rest of the day was memorable for an extra long nap in a very sweet state of a perfectly quiet mind.

On Tuesday, April 5th, at 9:45 am, I received some GREAT news! It was the results of my recent BMA. Luisa's email said that the report stated:

> No morphologic evidence of residual chronic lymphocystic leukemia; normocellular bone marrow, cellularity 30% with mild dysplasia noted in the peripheral blood, neutrophils and marrow which may be secondary to therapy.

In plain English, my bone marrow was clear and any minor blood abnormalities were related to treatment recovery. Luisa ended her email with, "Have a beautiful day!" Even though it was raining cats and dogs, my day was definitely beautiful, and made even more so when John and I received parental approval to surprise Syd and Aiden with a short visit that evening. As we tucked them in bed after they'd finished their homework and we'd played serious games of UNO and SKIP-BO, I butterfly kissed their foreheads, and reveled in the knowledge that my expiration date had just been bumped back, way back.

Arriving in the mail and dated April 11th , was another "Reconsent" packet of info from Dr. Sharman's office. I'd been pre-warned of its coming by Luisa, and her request for the prompt signing and returning of it was made clear by an attached note. Out of the 20 page document, seven pages had significantly new findings and warnings based on the results of patients' participation in the clinical trial. Some risks and side-effects like constipation and joint pain had moved from the common column to the very common column and some entirely new risks and side-effects had been added. They were sinus infections, physical weakness and lack of energy, musculoskeletal chest pain, baldness, red eye, colitis, flu, urinary tract infection, weight gain, squamous cell carcinoma, indigestion, cardiac failure, hemorrhoids, eczema and last but not least, oral herpes.

I don't know the exact number of patients in the BG study who were experiencing these ailments as a result of treatment, but the number was high enough to warrant my signature on the revised form as proof of my continued consent to carry out my three year contract. I signed my John Hancock in the space provided and hoped to God my remission wouldn't be plagued by these things, especially cardiac failure.

The day after I mailed in the Reconsent Form, I resumed my routine PET scans at OHSU, which had been put off because of the trial. Dr. Andersen continued to check for new or recurrent Merkel cell activity throughout my body and major organs and his clean bill of health from the most aggressive and deadly of skin cancers gave me great peace of mind. He was a firm believer in PET scans being more definitive than Merkel antibody tests of my blood in terms of finding cancer. The way I looked at it, two tests by experts in their fields were better than one.

Andersen called me the evening after my appointment, just as he'd promised and it was good news; no Merkel cancer was found anywhere. He wished me well and said to return in about 4-5 months for another PET and then off the cuff, added that his favorite homemade cookie was chocolate chip.

Andersen is a great doctor whose lack of subtlety adds to his charming bedside manner.

By the end of April I'd taught myself a lot about Neupogen, what exactly it was, how it worked and its side-effects, and after a blood test here in Salem showed my neutrophils going even lower, I contacted Dr. Sharman and Luisa about giving myself the shots. Although Sharman reiterated that such late neutropenia had been seen in other patients taking Gazyva, he said it was my call and if I wanted to do the shots he'd prescribe a 28 day supply. Two days later, off we went to WVCI to get the $150.00 drugs and learn how to deliver them by way of a poke in my stomach.

When we arrived, we went to the pharmacy and got my Neupogen, as well as a container in which to keep the drugs cold and a small disposal box with a red label stating, 'Medical- needle/sharp.' We then headed to a small room down the hallway and were met there by an infusion nurse. After introductions, she immediately took out one of the cold syringes already filled with the correct dosage and set it on a nearby table.

"Always store your Neupogen in the refrigerator at home and after taking it out allow about 30 minutes for each syringe to warm up before administration. You'll take the drug today, Wednesday, and Dr. Sharman wants you to take your next dosage on Thursday and then after that continue on a Monday/Thursday schedule."

"I understand."

"And either you or your husband can deliver the dosage to any fatty part of your skin, usually the stomach, upper arms or upper thighs/hip areas."

I glanced at my loving husband who had a, "Yes, I can do that, no I can't do that; yes I can do that, no I don't want to do that," look in his beautiful brown eyes. Immediately I responded with unbridled enthusiasm, "I WANT TO GIVE MYSELF THE SHOTS!"

"Are you sure?" John questioned me, ever so slightly.

"Absolutely! No doubt about it, Squirrel," I came back. "Look at the size of those needles, why they're super tiny. I'll hardly feel anything and I certainly have enough tummy fat to change poking spots."

While we waited for the first shot of Neupogen to reach room temperature, the nurse highlighted some of the most important information about its use. I needed to take it at the same time each day and not use the solution if it was cloudy, leaking or had changed color. Especially important was NO SHAKING OF THE SOLUTION and NO MISSING OF A DOSAGE.

Then she mentioned a few of the side effects; back, bone, and joint pain, cough, headache, upset stomach, and irritation at the shot site. Thankfully, my prescription pamphlet was very thorough so I didn't need total recall of everything she'd shared. My Neupogen dosage had warmed up enough for its injection and I was ready for action.

"Where do you want to put it?" the nurse calmly asked me.

"Well, I think my tummy is the place to start. I have plenty of fat there and can see it with no trouble. I figure I can pinch some together with my left hand and hold the syringe with my right.

"Sounds like a winner," chimed in John, appearing a bit uncomfortable.

"This is what I want you to do. Grab the fat on one side of your belly button between your left thumb and fingers. Then with the syringe held between your index and middle fingers and top of the plunger balanced against your thumb, poke your skin decisively by inserting the needle all the way in. Slowly push the plunger down until all the liquid has been delivered. Then, keep your finger on the plunger while you remove the needle and once totally out, gently let go of your skin."

"That's exactly what I watched over and over again on the YouTube channel. No problemo," I said with total confidence.

"Okay, let's have you do it," she said.

"Gottcha," I came back.

"You can do this," encouraged my husband, always my personal cheerleader.

I placed the syringe in my right hand and grabbed tummy fat in my left and plunged the needle at a good poking site. The Neupogen was delivered in under three seconds, without any foul-ups and only a smidgen of pain. To be completely honest though, I didn't relish the notion of jabbing a needle into my belly two times a week, no matter how small the delivery device was.

A few days later, after only two shots at home, my CBC blood test at Salem Clinic showed my neutrophil count was normal. Sharman said to stop the injections and see if the count would hold on its own. It did. As usual, he'd been right to suggest I give my body the time it needed to bounce back on its own. My lack of patience cost me $150.00 since I couldn't get my money back on the unused Neupogen. I did learn an important lesson, however, and that was how to shoot myself in the stomach and maybe that would come in handy some day.

May, June, and July of 2016, were problem free months and I was really feeling good; no set- backs whatsoever. I was following all the advice I'd heard from the experts about washing my hands constantly, keeping away from people who were sick, wearing my UV clothing when in the sun, going to see Dr. Sharman every 3 months for blood tests and exams, getting plenty of rest and sleep, taking vitamins and drinking green tea. I was the model of what a post clinical trial CLL patient should be. Then came early August and that's when we decided to take Syd and Aiden to McMinnville's prime fun spot, Wings and Waves Water Park, definitely not our best decision of the summer.

The cost of tickets weren't as high as my Neupogen shots, but still very expensive. The advantage was the purchase price enabled us to enjoy everything for a full day, not just a few hours. Hurrying into our swimsuits, we emerged from the locker rooms to take in 10 glorious water slides, an enormous wave pool that mimicked the ocean, a real Boeing 747 aircraft hanging from the roof of the place and much, much more. I was on overload and wondered what to do first.

"Grandma, will you be my tube partner and go down the big slide?" asked a very excited grand-daughter.

Not pausing to contemplate my decision, I exclaimed, "YES!"

Aiden asked John the same question and quickly we became a four-some climbing the tall, crowded staircase to the underbelly of the Boeing. It took us 45 minutes to reach our launch pad and when the employee announced, "Go," Syd and I zoomed down the slide. For the first couple seconds all was good and then I made a terrible mistake.

Thinking we were too far to one side on our big inner tube, I tried to adjust my position in back so we could steer better. When I did, I jerked my left shoulder with such force it felt as if a bolt of lightning suddenly surged through my joint. Immediately I knew I'd done something really, really stupid and all thoughts of me feeling good during my three years of CLL follow-up went out the window.

Being a grandparent is doing one's best to make every day with grandkids a good one. So for the next four hours I soldiered through, pretending to have fun while my entire shoulder was crying out in pain. Nothing seemed broken and no bones stuck out at strange angles, but I was pretty sure what I had was no run of the mill weekend booboo. After we took the grandkids home and John and I were in the car alone I spilled the beans about my shoulder.

"It's a little late, but when we're home I want you to lie down and we'll ice the spot and get you some Tylenol. Wish we had some left over Vicodin from your Merkel surgery," my husband bemoaned.

"You and me both," I quickly came back.

In short order, I was diagnosed with 2 good sized tears in my left rotator cuff and required a shot of cortisone to manage the very painful 12 sessions of physical therapy. The good news though, is I recovered close to 95% use and rotation of my shoulder and learned never again to fuck up my state of well being with things that could put me at risk of taking it all away. Cancer is all about risk versus reward and so are giant water slides.

My sweet friend Char Andrews once told me as she was dying of breast cancer what in life worried her the most. She said that it was being hit by a bus! That the fight against cancer was more than enough for her to take on, and she didn't need to add more opponents, especially those that were accidental. She said it's important to soak up the respites from cancer, no matter how short they might be; they were like gift certificates and all of them would be out of date some day. Charlene Matthews died four years after being diagnosed with stage 4 breast cancer, all the while working tirelessly to help pass what in the end she didn't need to utilize, Oregon's "Death With Dignity" legislation. I think about her a lot and wish so much she could have survived the Big C.

I'm very thankful I live in a state that helps people avoid the pain and suffering of a slow death; that allows individuals the choice of time and circumstance of their own passing. If some believe this is wrong, then let them cross over as they choose, but don't force their belief systems onto others.

The end of August, with my rotator cuff feeling a lot better, was our first Summit Art Fair which played out on Karin and Drew's driveway. I publicized the event by way of Facebook, large neon signs with balloons displayed everywhere, emails to friends and relatives, the 'Garage Sale' section of our local newspapers, and of course the most old-fashioned of ways, word of mouth.

When the Saturday arrived, Syd manned her toy cash register, and Aiden took charge of the free lemonade and cookies, sampling them often for quality assurance. John and I arranged all the sale items nicely on 8 long tables, with small shoulder purses and scarves over-flowing 3 large coat racks. The kiddos had made $1.00 'goodie bags', each full of pencils, erases, stickers, whistles, post-it-notes, Hershey kisses and homemade slime inside plastic Easter eggs. Both grandkids agreed that young shoppers were a large part of our target audience and usually had money to spare so the bags would definitely sell well. A big jar decorated with pictures of adoptable dogs and cats sat next to the cash register, encouraging customers to not only buy, but donate.

Things went better than expected all day and by closing time we'd brought in more than my co-pay for a Neulesta shot, not counting the jar stuffed with ten and twenty dollar bills. We drove to the Humane Society and happily handed over all the money, and because the sweet lady at reception liked our jar, we gave it to her. Driving home we were giddy with the feeling that we'd done something important, something important AND something good.

September and October moved by swiftly, with the 2016 presidential election set for November 8th. Like the other 65,844,610 Americans, I wanted Hillary to win, but in our democracy the candidate with the most number of citizens voting for him/her, doesn't decide the outcome of the most important election in the United States.

Hillary won the popular vote, while Mr. Trump won the electoral college, something that might be eliminated someday, just as in years past so was slavery, refusing women the vote and denying marriage based on sexual orientation. We had a new president and I hoped he'd do well.

What was so unusual about the evening of the 8th wasn't just the election results, but how suddenly that night it dawned on me that the further away I got from the end of my BG chemo treatments in August of 2015, the closer I got to needing treatment again. Three years is what Sharman hoped for in terms of my CLL remission and I'd already passed the one year mark by two months. Every day and month I felt good was terrific, but those days and months also meant bad lymphocytes were growing in my blood, planning their next assault.

With my breast and Merkel cancers, hitting the five year mark from treatment was wonderful because it indicated the diseases could really be gone. With leukemia, more time away from treatment simply means I'm creeping toward another round of treatment to buy me more time. No wonder the saying by Sally Kempton that reads, "It's hard to fight an enemy who has outposts in your head," applies aptly to my way of thinking about Chronic Lymphocytic Leukemia. No wonder the moments of me having a 'quiet mind' are far and few between.

On November 28th, John had his hip replacement surgery and our roles as patient and care-giver suddenly reversed. I tended to his needs and tried hard to keep his spirits up when he struggled with daily activities and issues of mobility and pain management. As always, Sydney and Aiden were the best medicine, but having Grandpa elevating his leg on the couch was a whole lot worse than having Grandma protecting

Billy Jean in the Courthouse swimming pool.

John had always been the more physical playmate; not me, and now the kiddos weren't even supposed to sit on his lap or play indoor nerf basketball with the Squirrel. The adjustment was hard and made me realize how tough it must have been for him when I couldn't do things because I felt lousy or so fatigued all I wanted to do was crawl under a blanket, close my eyes and block out the world.

Fortunately, Syd and Aiden learned to switch gears and find things Grandpa could do that wouldn't be bad for him. Things like "I Spy With My Little Eye,' Tick Tac Toe, doing puzzles and drawing pictures. They cuddled carefully on the couch next to him and were at his beck and call for fresh ice water, Peppermint Patties and the TV remote. They smothered him with hugs and kisses and all the reasons he needed to get better fast.

By Christmas Eve, John was walking with a cane, and only used one crutch to go up and down our stairs. Me, well I had another great appointment with Dr. Sharman on December 29th and my blood work showed my remission was holding strong with a low lymphocyte count and everything else as it should be. For one year I was in remission, sweet, sweet remission.

MILEPOST 2017

In January of 2017, Donald J. Trump was sworn in as President of the United States, a real surprise for many learned pollsters and countless Americans and most world leaders. The next day millions of people, mostly female, marched in the streets of America to protest his taking over of the reins of our country's leadership from Barak Obama. Salem held a march and I was proud to be a part of it, to be part of something much greater than myself. In many ways that march was like being part of the clinical trial I'd joined over a year ago. Both took on huge challenges and sadly both might have failed, but the celebration came in the trying.

February and March were wrought, not with the perils of leukemia, but rather the many realities of growing older. Small cysts on my head and other places had grown larger, my eyesight had deteriorated and future cataract surgery wasn't so "future" anymore, ancient fillings and crowns were cracking and the little aches and pains of daily living demanded longer and longer periods of recovery. These were all minor complaints, but I was pissed anyway, that is until company came to visit and handed me something to REALLY be pissed about.

Letting down my CLL guard, out of town in-laws wanted to stay for a few days and assured me they were in tip top shape health wise...no recent ills that might be still lingering just an ity bity, no present fevers, sniffles, coughs, sore throats, not a single thing to worry about. I'd explained my vulnerability to infections and had their assurance they had no germs to spread. So I made an executive decision and, wanting to be the best of hosts, trusted their word and gave them my bedroom while I took the couch.

It took only 1 day after their 3 day stay that I was running a temperature of 101.8 degrees, suffering terrible pressure in my sinuses and owning a horrible sore throat. A brief phone call verified they too were a little under the weather, but only a "tiny" bit, while me, well I was drowning in their forecast. Later one person confided she thought she was over her "touch of something" before they arrived; apparently not. So much for having visitors and me trusting their clean bill of health. And me giving them my bedroom to turn it into one giant Petri dish that a spic and span cleaning immediately after their departure couldn't even handle.

Next time Keizer's Comfort Inn would be their home base, and if needed, I'd kick in some money to help if they were short on funds. After all, I shouldn't have been so naïve to risk their visit in the first place, guarantees by them or not. Yes, it was time to put my health needs first; I was going to have to be selfish to stay well and alive.

John and I rushed to Sharman's office and saw Pat, his excellent PA. She applauded me for my quick action, unlike the whole Allopurinal incident during which time I waited way too long and almost got sepsis. Pat started me on 250 mg of Azithromycin, STAT! She also explained that it was her educated guess that what I was experiencing was my personal CLL's infection of choice.

"Because you've had repeated, though not regular, sinus infections since your leukemia diagnosis rather than bouts of pneumonia, UTI's, or other things, I think this is how your body can be expected to first react when your immune system is attacked."

"Is that a good thing?" I asked.

"Well, your symptoms are like an early warning system. And early warning symptoms aren't a bad thing." She paused briefly and then added cautiously, "If I were you, from now on I'd have all out of town guests stay in nearby motels. Remember, prevention is a whole lot smarter than treatment after the damage has already been done."

"I get it," was my contrite response, with a mental note to myself to check the rates at the Comfort Inn.

I wasn't surprised a short time later when Luisa emailed me the results of the blood work done during my unscheduled visit with Pat and my lymphocyte count was up; infections do that, especially to people with my disease. I was surprised though when I noticed a category that I only remembered being done year's earlier by my first oncologist, Dr. John Strother. The type of test is called "Immunology" and being the astute record keeper I've always been, I found my February, 2011, results and compared them to my now, February, 2017, numbers. What a difference! And it wasn't a good difference; no, it was far from it.

The test measures the level of antibodies, also known as immunoglobulins (Ig) in my blood. These antibodies are substances made by my body's immune system in response to bacteria, viruses, fungus, animal dander, or cancer cells. Antibodies attach to the foreign substances so immune systems can destroy them. My immune system, unfortunately, makes low levels of these antibodies so I have a greater chance of developing repeated infections, and in my specific case, infections of my sinuses.

There are five major types of antibodies, with three of them being VERY important to me with CLL; IgA, IgG and IgM. IgA antibodies are found in areas of the body such as nose, breathing passages, digestive tract, ears, eyes, and vagina. IgG antibodies are found in all body fluids and are very important in fighting bacterial and viral infections. IgM antibodies are the largest antibody. They are found in blood and lymph fluid and are the first type of antibody made in response to an infection. They also cause other immune system cells to destroy foreign substances. Therefore, the levels of these antibodies are a big deal in terms of my leukemia and my ability to stay healthy.

The normal range of these three antibodies vary greatly: IgA is 70-400 mg/dl, IgG is 700-1600mg/dl and IgM is 40-230 mg/dl. In 2011, my respective levels were 47, 596 and 43. Those were not good levels and now in 2017, my levels were a lot worse with IgA being 13, IgG, 306 and IgM less than 8. How in the world could I feel so good, have very few infections and end up with test results like that? Was I a walking, talking contradiction to medical science or miracle of human nature? The truth is I'm neither.

Luisa, after talking at length with Dr. Sharman, informed me that my other immune functions like neutrophil counts were normal and therefore my body still had adequate ways to help fight off illnesses, not all illnesses, but a good share of them. So even though my immunoglobulins were heading south, things would only become serious if I experienced repeated infections within a short period of time and if each required antibiotics over and over again. Sadly, I knew infections would most likely be the grim reaper if my remission didn't buy me enough time for doctors to find a cure. I was feeling good though after my Z Pack did the trick, and the good weather of spring was just around the corner. Then, out of nowhere, in early June, our sweet kitty Charlie got real sick and my good feelings were brought to a close.

I'd found him well over 10 years ago hiding under the abandoned house next door and after months of generous feedings and soft coaxing, he finally emerged and ventured into our yard for some cautious pets. We slowly domesticated him, and eventually he became a loving member of our family.

In mid-June, he began losing his appetite and then had constant diarrhea with black and bloody feces. My little boy was in a lot of pain and I rushed him to the vet where a large mass was discovered in his lower bowel. I was faced with the decision of subjecting him to harsh invasive tests which would likely diagnose an inoperable cancerous tumor and cause death in a few weeks, or letting him be put to sleep. I chose to end his life peacefully while he lay in my arms. To this day I can see his face at the patio door and hear his meow to come in and join me on my lap. The pain of his loss forever lingers and will always hurt more than any of the side-effects of the clinical trial.

My labs and visit with Sharman and Luisa on June 27th went well but I was having a terrible time adjusting to the new Eugene location of WVCI and Dr. Sharman's office. I mourned the loss of Springfield's spacious, beautifully decorated clinic, with the rolling hills outside the huge wall of windows, and my beloved horse grazing in her pasture. Eugene's quarters were sterile and cramped and I felt boxed in; trapped and lonely without my constant companion.

The new blood draw room was small, with technicians and patients working hard to stay out of each others' way, weaving back and forth like go carts on a track having a hard time preventing crashes. It was apparent the stress and adjustment of the move had been especially hard on the medical staff; their faces couldn't lie, even though their positive remarks tried to cover up the truth.

On a good note though, my lymphocyte numbers were still in the low range at 0.62 and my infection-fighting neutrophils were good. The IgG level hadn't dipped much lower and if I hadn't just lost Charlie and my horse, I would have proffered a grin at all the news. Clearly, I was still in remission at two years! Any real celebration; however, was tempered by warnings of many more CLL patients experiencing secondary skin cancers than first suspected.

"Are you still testing for Merkel antibodies in your blood?" asked a serious Dr. Sharman.

"Yes, every three months I have my blood drawn at Salem Clinic and they send it off to the University of Washington as part of Dr. Nghiem's research into Merkel carcinoma. So far so good; I've been negative for four years now. And I still have at least a yearly PET scan at OHSU because Dr. Andersen wants to make very sure no cancer has come back or that I've developed a new one. Being thorough is one of the things I like best about him...and you." Sharman flashed me a 'Thank you.'

"You know," I confessed, "It hasn't been the breast cancer or even the CLL that's changed my life the most; it's the Merkel. I used to love the sun; loved playing tennis in it, doing yard work in it, walking on the beach in it and best of all swimming in water warmed by it. Now I try to avoid that ball of fire, like a vampire avoids daylight."

"I'm sorry," said Luisa who sat by Sharman updating my chart with new vitals and test results.

"It's not like I can't enjoy a sunny day, but the precautions are what get to me sometime; the constant putting on of sun block and UV clothing to cover my body and hats to make sure sun doesn't shine on my face." Turning lemons into lemonade I added, "On a bright note, it's better to be alive without a tan than in the ground with one." Again, John was the only person in the room who seemed to enjoy my dark sense of humor.

When July rolled around, the kiddos and me pulled together another Summit Art Fair to raise money for the Willamette Humane Society. Being seasoned crafters by now and with experience at putting on such an endeavor, things went smoothly. As before, Sydney manned the play cash register and Aiden the refreshment table. They were definitely learning the business side of business; provide your customers with free food, well made products sold by friendly workers at reasonable prices, and money would be made. Also, there might be left-over Snickerdoodles and strawberry-lemonade!

On August 21st, me and millions of other people across the United States, watched something extraordinary occur, a total solar eclipse. It was a once in a lifetime experience and my hubby and I viewed it from our beach in the backyard. I slathered myself in Neutrogena broad spectrum SPF 70 and wore my UV SKINZ hat with the extra wide brim atop my head and approved eclipse glasses covered my eyes.

Ever so slowly, the Sun, Moon and Earth aligned perfectly and day turned into night, the temperature dropped and our sand turned cold. Through my glasses I watched the Sun's corona and surface features of the Moon; stars and planets became visible. I picked up a handful of sand and let the grains slip slowly between my fingers, realizing again I was but a single life in the whole world of time.

September 25th was another appointment with Sharman and my usual blood draw. Surprisingly, two of my Ig levels had improved. I was at 323.57 for my IgG and 23.62 for my IgM; IgA stayed pretty much the same. I expected my lymphocyte count to be low and it was at .87; very minor changes in other counts had occurred, but nothing suspicious or worrisome noted Sharman and Luisa.

My days were moving quickly and happily with lots of kiddo time after school, soccer matches on the weekends, lunches with friends, tennis, and of course hanging out with the love of my life, John. I was ME again and even with occasional reminders of having leukemia, I was feeling GREAT! In fact, I was feeling so good, I was starting to forget how lousy I'd once felt.

November 7th was my appointment in Portland with my Merkel surgeon, and the PET scan showed I was still free of that cancer. With four years remission under my belt, the chances of Merkel recurrence were slighter and slighter. Dr. Andersen recommended just one more scan the following year and that would be it; 'unless' and that was a 'BIG unless', some change in my health deemed a future scan necessary. I chose not to question my future and we left his office by noon and got home to Keizer around 12:45.

November and December of 2017, were wonderful months with more and more grand-kid time. Something that's so great about getting to see your grandkids often, such as we do, is it's like living with someone before you marry them. You see the REAL them; not just the VISITING them. We've seen Sydney and Aiden when they've been happy and when they've been sad and all the emotions in between. We've had to say "No" to them when they've wanted a "Yes," and we've all had time to talk about and understand the why's of our answers. They've started serious conversations and we've listened to them without moving on to more pressing agendas; our relationships aren't rushed and forced into a time sensitive play date with Grandma or Grandpa. I sympathize greatly with Grandparents who live far away from their grandkids; it would break my heart if we did.

December 13th was the date I met my old tennis partner, Donna, for a holiday lunch at Love, Love, Teriyaki. We were good friends and she was someone who could always be counted on to captain a team when nobody else wanted the responsibility, or let's be blunt, the headache. She'd been after me to get back into the sport competitively, but even though I'd been playing socially, I was still hesitant to commit. I didn't want to say yes and then have to drop out like I'd had to do with breast cancer, Merkel, and most recently, when CLL stuffed my spleen with bad lymphocytes.

"How you feeling Pam?" she asked gently while we sipped tea and I gave up on my chopsticks for an American fork.

"Good," I said, feeling a bit uneasy about saying so. "Knock on wood," I added, tapping our table on its top.

"So glad to hear that. When's your next doctor visit?"

"One week from today, but it'll be with Sharman's PA, Pat, because he'll be out of town. I really like her; she's smart, nice, and takes good care of me."

"Been getting a lot of grandkid time?" Donna changed the discussion from medical to personal.

"As much as we can. They're very happy to see Grandma is her old self at long last. And that they can hug me without squishing anything they shouldn't." Rocking back in our chairs, we both let out hearty laughs.

"I'm back to walking two miles, three times a week, swimming at the Courthouse, hitting with John and really starting to get back in shape. Never thought I'd be doing those things again, but I've finally got the energy and the desire." A very pregnant pause followed and then I added, "Might be ready to get back into tennis 100%, under the right circumstances."

"Well, it just so happens I'm putting together a +65 womens' team and I'd like nothing better than you and me partnering up. How does that sound?" She was excited to say the words and I was excited to hear them.

"I'd really like that...Hirt and Johnson together again; sounds pretty darn good. But I'm worried about a few things."

"Okay, let's hear what's bothering you."

I spoke slowly and clearly, "I'd like to pay guest fees instead of officially joining the club until I know for sure my body is up for serious play. It's been a long time since I've really run around on a court slamming a ball. Thank God, I got my rating lowered from 3.5 to 3.0, or I wouldn't even try being on a team at all. Something else too, I'd want to make sure our matches are inside because the sun and I are not on speaking terms any more and never will be again."

"Gotcha," Donna said immediately. "You let me take care of your first worry, about the guest fees, and the second problem isn't a problem at all. We start team practice in January, all inside, and our season runs from April through June, all inside. And the best part; if we reach sectionals, they're inside at Tacoma, WA, November 1-4."

"Count me in!" I exclaimed, wondering how in the world my partner was going to solve problem number one, and me scared stiff that I was no near ready to hit with an official team.

December 20th arrived and we cruised down Interstate 5 to my last clinical trial appointment for 2017. Pat and Luisa were their usual wonderful selves during my visit and my numbers were where they should be for me, holding steady. Besides my numbers being good, I hadn't encountered more sinus infections, all lymph nodes were declared normal and not enlarged, blood pressure read at a nice 135/70, temperature charted its course at 98.6 and PET and Merkel blood tests remained both negative.

Hopefully 2018, would go even better.

MILEPOST 2018

My 2018, commenced just after midnight on New Year's Eve, with Whistling Pete's screeching in the street outside my bedroom window while inside I struggled to get much needed shut eye. I don't like fireworks as an adult and only tolerated them as a kid. To me they're a damn annoyance. They keep people awake who want to sleep; they scare animals off into the night; they pollute our water, land and air, and their fleeting pleasure is at the cost of a whole lot of money for a little while of fun. Not a real good return on anyone's investment, that is unless you're paying off a porn star so you can win an election.

With my quiet night a thing of the past, I went to my calendar next to the computer to check how the first month of a new year was looking. A lovely colonoscopy was scheduled for Monday, the 8th, with Dr. Hoda, strictly routine; Merkel blood drawn on Martin Luther King Day, the 15th; the second Women's March at our State Capitol on Saturday, the 21st. I highlighted those things with a bright yellow marker and circled in green my tennis times at Salem Tennis and Swim Club. I was returning to my beloved sport, full time.

January passed quickly and before I knew it February arrived and I was staring my 70th birthday in the face, the face of a woman whose Merkel scares had finally faded into her laugh lines. My body was feeling good but my mind was yelling, 'Stop putting off things you've always wanted to do, Pam. Carpe diem, carpe diem!"

It was time for me to examine what I REALLY wanted to do NOW, while I still could. If cancer does nothing else to a life, it speeds up the living of it. Days were good, numbers were holding, so I was primed to get going on number one of my Bucket List, a visit to Washington DC and a tour of the White House. John was completely supportive and my grandkids were thrilled when I told them.

"Do you think you'll get to see the President?" Aiden asked.

"Well, he's a very busy man so I don't think so," I answered.

"Maybe when he's not busy and playing golf, you can see him," was Syd's solution to POTUS's full schedule at 1600 Pennsylvania Avenue.

I had a routine check up with my Primary Care Physician, Dr. Wang, on March 5th, to bring him up to speed on all my recent blood tests and visits with Sharman. When told about my upcoming travels to D.C. with a good friend, he wrote me out another prescription for Azithromycin to have on hand and emphasized again the common sense precautions for CLL patients. Before my parting, he strongly recommended I contact Sharman about getting the new FDA approved shingles vaccination now available to people like me who couldn't have vaccines made by way of a live virus. He explained things this way.

"Shingrix (recombinant zoster vaccine), reduces the risk of shingles by more than 85% in people like you, Pam, and you can get it whether or not you remember having had chickenpox as a kid. Chickenpox and shingles are related because they're caused by the same virus and after somebody recovers from chickenpox, the virus stays dormant in the body, but can reactivate years later and cause shingles. Shingles is bad, especially for leukemia patients whose bodies can't really handle infections like they used to, whether you're in remission or not. This new shot has a good chance of preventing something you definitely don't want to get." His usual jovial demeanor had been replaced with serious concern for my well-being.

"What are the side-effects like?" was my time honored query.

"None have been real serious in any of the clinical trials; just the usual things like a sore arm where the shot is given, along with possible redness and swelling; also, you might feel a little tired, have some muscle pain, perhaps a headache, shivering, fever, stomach pain or a touch of nausea. These symptoms go away on their own in about two to three days, but trust me, these are nothing compared to coming down with shingles." He made a note of our conversation on his laptop and then turned my way again.

"I'll contact Dr. Sharman or my clinical trial nurse Luisa and see what they advise me to do," I said.

"Good idea. Glad you'll check into this," he stated as we both stood up to end our visit. "And it's wonderful to see you doing so well."

"Yea, the trial was sure worth it," I smiled. Walking down the hallway toward the lobby I said "Hi" to Loretta, one of his nurses who'd been a student of mine years ago at South Salem High School.

"Hi Mrs. Johnson," she warmly greeted her old English Lit teacher.

"Loretta, I think it's time you called me Pam, okay?"

"I'll try Mrs. Johnson, errrr, I mean Pam."

"Good. And another thing; you feel free to let me know if the doctor ever gives you a hard time and if he does, he and I will have a little talk." My solemn expression and strong teacher voice gave weight to my words and took Loretta aback.

Then I added rather innocently, "Bye Dr. Wang," as he stood silently a few feet behind my student. "You both have a nice day."

"We will," he laughed. "We will," followed Loretta, a huge grin on her face.

The next morning I contacted Sharman and he gave me the go ahead for the Shingles vaccines and I made arrangements for the two dosages. In no time at all, I received my first shot at Safeway pharmacy and at the same time picked up my infection fighting antibiotic. Being proactive with my own health was like hitting the sweet spot of my tennis racket...both felt sooooooooooo gooooood.

Donna and I planned carefully for our trip, and I made sure I read, THE HIDDEN WHITE HOUSE...Harry Truman and the Reconstruction of American's Most Famous Residence by Robert Klara. I didn't want to simply tour the White House; I wanted to understand some of its history. Not knowing for sure if I'd get a second chance to travel to DC, other sites I wanted to take in were the Washington Monument, The National Archives, The Museum of Natural History, the Lincoln Memorial, The Newseum, Arlington Cemetery and the National Museum of African American History and Culture. These few were carefully chosen because neither of us wanted to cram too much into our seven day visit. We didn't want to rush; we wanted to savor an experience. Actually see and take in the 'Declaration of Independence' not simply walk by it and notice how old the parchment it was written on was.

My April 5th labs and appointment with Dr. Sharman revealed I continued to be in remission. True, I was a bit low in the lymphocyte numbers and total protein, as well as my IgG, IgA and IgM counts, but with CLL I'd learned a long time ago that it was always how patients' FEEL and not the numbers that were most important. John, Sharman, Luisa and I were all smiles that morning as we said our good-byes and continued on with our Thursday. Only one thing would have made my visit more perfect and that was if out WVCI's window I could still buddy up with my pretty horse.

In May my number 1 Bucket List "want to" happened, an unforgettable time in Washington D.C. with one of my best friends who just so happened to have an amazing lob and drop shot. Being in a brand new place didn't scare me like I thought it might, far from it. Instead, I felt brave, courageous and bold as I took on the risk of distancing myself from the sanctuary of home. Chronic Lymphocytic Leukemia was far, far away, not because I was in remission, but because I was so full of everything I was experiencing. And the Uber driver from Somalia who played African music and talked about saving up to bring his family to America was right up there with standing next to President Kennedy's grave and watching the eternal light flicker in the breeze.

When July rolled around it was back to Dr. Sharman for labs, an exam and consult. It was my last, yes, my final appointment with him as part of my three year Bendamustine/Gazyva clinical trial follow-up and it was bittersweet. He was more than my doctor; he'd become my friend, someone I could let down my guard with and trust to take good care of me. He was my 'go to' guy and his staff was always only a phone call away whenever I had a problem or needed someone to talk with. The trial had put me at the front of the line for personal care and now I had to join the masses of patients vying for attention in a swamped health care system. My eyes welled with tears.

"Sorry," I told Dr. Sharman, tears rolling down my cheeks. "I don't want to stop coming here. You make me feel safe, and I don't want to lose that feeling."

Wiping away my tears I added, "That probably sounds crazy, huh?"

"Not crazy at all, Pam," Sharman replied. "Just remember, Dr. Strother in Salem is a very good doctor and knows a lot about CLL. And when you need treatment again, I'd like to help decide which kind is best for you. Of course if that's alright."

"That'd be more than alright with me," I responded without hesitation. Pausing slightly, I couldn't stop myself from asking, "With my blood work still looking good except for my low Ig levels, how long do you think I could stay in remission?"

"Well, that's the million dollar question, isn't it? You've reached the three year mark and that was our first goal. I don't see you feeling good changing anytime soon so my best advice is to go about your life and do the things you love." Sharman looked at me and seemed to ready himself for my response.

"I don't want to sound ungrateful, but the first year was pretty rough. It took me quite a while to get my strength back and start feeling like my old self again. I guess what I really want is more **good** time before more **treatment** time."

"And I really think you'll get what you want, but I don't know exactly how much of what you want." His voice sounded encouraging, but a little sad too. We were the only two in the room with my John home nursing a bad calf injury and Luisa helping a new clinical trial patient. I didn't remember us ever being alone before and the room felt huge.

He broke our silence by saying, "There's two oral drugs that you, me and Strother should consider when your CLL remission ends and treatment is deemed necessary. One is Imbruvica and an even newer, but FDA approved targeted therapy, called Venetoclax. They aren't without side effects, but research shows many patients have handled them well and results, they've been very good. And remember, newer and better drugs are coming out all the time for Chronic Lymphocytic Leukemia. And let's hope for a cure, soon."

"At least with pills I won't need pokes as often," I chuckled.

"A word to the wise though," Sharman turned even more serious than he already was. "Make sure Imbruvica and Venclexta are on the drug formulary list of whatever Medicare insurance plan or supplement you have. They're expensive and you'll want all the help you can get paying for them."

Our time was up and I handed him three cards. Each had a different name on the envelope…one was Dr. Sharman, one Luisa and one, Pat.

"You didn't have to do this," he said a bit uncomfortably. "You're the one who took all the risks during the trial and went through all we asked of you. You did the real work."

I gave him the cards and a hug, and went out into reception where I signed forms giving permission to him and Willamette Valley Cancer Institute and Research Center to fax all my medical records over to Dr. John Strother at Salem Oncology Specialists. Then I put on one of the masks I always carried in my purse and walked in, for the first time, to the chemotherapy treatment area that was now located in Eugene instead of Springfield.

No one looked familiar, not any nurses who administered the drugs, not assistants who took vitals, not any patients or anyone visiting them; it was strange to me and I was a stranger to it. On my way out I suddenly noticed a large framed picture on the wall. It was my horse! There she was, just as pretty as I remembered her, the friend who'd helped me get through all 6 months of the clinical trial. Below her picture was her name, "Blondie" and a sentence explaining she was an American Quarter Horse that for over a decade had been a show horse. Blondie was being honored, not for "show," but for the constant and healing presence she provided to the many cancer patients who underwent chemotherapy in order to live longer and better lives. And I was one of those patients.

"Blondie," I said to myself. "What a pretty name for such a wonderful horse. I'll never forget you, my friend."

Late in August I got my second shingles shot and like the first, suffered only the minor side-effects of redness and soreness at the injection site. I also visited my dermatologist for a routine, all body skin examination and was relieved that no new areas of suspicion were found. With skin cancers being the number 1 secondary cancer among CLL patients, I never went to Dr. Hale without expecting some kind of bad news. Getting older and my skin resembling more and more a "connect the dots game", it was hard for me to stay current with my own outer layer so getting regular check-ups were very important.

September 10th found me at Cascade Hall on the grounds of the Oregon State Fair, checking out new Medicare programs because my old one had been discontinued. Remembering what Dr. Sharman had said about the possibility of future CLL treatments focusing on the drugs Imbruvica and Venclexta, I searched a variety of plans with different drug formularies and then zeroed in on the ones which provided me those medications and allowed ME to choose my own doctors. In addition, the plan had to have an out of pocket cap and reasonable monthly premiums.

I have a Masters Degree in Education, real life experience as a Technical Writer and 70 years of practical experience as a human being and still I wanted to pull my hair out listening to all the folks touting the wonders of **their** Medicare plan over someone else's. People my age are supposed to be enjoying their golden years, not having heart palpitations because programs are so complicated it'd take Stephen Hawkins to figure out the darn things. Eventually, after hours of research, I chose Providence Medicare Advantage, Flex Group Plan + Rx and hoped I made the right decision. My CLL care depended on it.

September 29th, 2018, was the perfect day for soccer. Both Aiden and Sydney had their Saturday games at the Capitol Futball Complex in Salem and John and I were both there to cheer them on. We opened up our chairs next to Karin while Drew got his boys warmed up and ready to go. Aiden followed his father's directions carefully, standing out in the group because of his small size and head of long golden curls flopping over his face while his headband circled his neck.

"Suppose Sydney is already warming up with her team?" I questioned my daughter.

"Ya, they're doing drills next to the turf field," she replied quietly.

Mothers can sense sadness in their children even when everyone around them misses it and my radar is especially strong when Karin isn't side by side with happy go lucky, Drew. I glanced her way as Aiden dribbled down the field after taking the ball away from an opponent. My child was fighting back tears at the same time she cheered for her son. In an instant I knew she must be thinking about Maryn.

Maryn was the 7 year old sister of Syd's teammate, Cora. This sweet little girl had been diagnosed with the same kind of brain cancer, glioblastoma, that'd taken the life of Senator John McCain of Arizona. A clinical trial was found for her in Cincinnati, Ohio, offering hope that she might live longer than the usual life expectancy of 6 months. But Maryn's body couldn't tolerate the drugs, and more MRI's showed aggressive tumor growth throughout her brain. She and her family left Ohio and returned home.

Karin handed me her cell phone and I read the most recent email about Maryn. A few nights ago she'd woken up vomiting and having seizures, and she couldn't swallow or talk. She was taken first to Salem Hospital and then quickly transferred to Dornbeckers Children's Hospital in Portland. By Wednesday she'd bounced back a little and was able to go home. She left the hospital with anti-seizure medication and steroids to help control her brain swelling. The best that could be done now was handling her symptoms and making her as comfortable as possible. Maryn was given just two months to live.

As Aiden got the ball back and made another pass to a teammate who kicked it over the goalie's head, I looked up from the email, heartbroken. I thought about my last conversation with Sharman and the greed I expressed for wanting more remission time than three years. That was wrong; I should have been expressing appreciation for my 1,095 "bonus" days of life. The success of my trial was so unfair in comparison to the failure of Maryn's.

As Aiden's game ended and Syd's was about to begin, a large group of people formed a circle on the sidelines around a stroller with a little girl inside. It was Maryn. She was all bundled in warm clothing and blankets, her thinning brown hair covered by a small felt hat pulled down over her ears. The group were all those who loved her; her mom and dad, grandparents, aunts and uncles, cousins and best friends. They'd all gathered to celebrate not only a day in the life of a little girl who always found great joy in living, but to also celebrate Cora who was on the field playing her heart out so Maryn could cheer her on one more time.

September left slowly and October arrived and I returned to the care of Dr. John Strother in Salem at Oregon Oncology Specialists. His 4th floor area reminded me of Springfield's Willamette Valley Cancer Institute, big comfortable chairs, fresh flowers in pretty vases, magazines and same day newspapers lying on coffee and end tables, pretty pictures on the walls and automatic flush toilets. The only thing missing was a picture window with my Blondie outside.

"Please take a seat, Pam," the receptionist said. "Trina, Dr. Strother's nurse, will be out soon to get you." Another oncology office and another person already calling me by my first name.

"Hi, Pam," Trina said as she came over. She hadn't changed in five years, the same lovely figure and hair pulled back in a youthful pony tail. Full of energy for a Monday morning appointment at 7:45 am, she took me to an exam room where I was weighed, had my blood pressure and oxygen levels checked, as well as my temperature. We exchanged some small talk about how life had been treating us since we'd last spoken and before heading out the door mentioned that Dr. Sharman's office hadn't faxed my records over yet.

"Don't worry," she stated. "I'm on the top of the situation and will make sure we get them soon.

I nodded her my thanks, resettled my bottom in the chair, finished the last of my Smart Water and checked my silenced cell for emails and texts. The doctor knocked gently before entering and we smiled at one another, happy to reconnect again. Strother was still lean and handsome, a snappy dresser who liked bold colored ties and cool, name-brand sneakers. The hair on his balding head was grayer, but that added to his distinguished appearance. We shook hands.

"How have things been going?" he asked in his friendly manner.

"Good," I replied. "At least I'm still here."

I brought him up to speed on my health situations, both CLL and Merkel, as well as the fun stuff like grandkids and tennis.

"And how are your three boys?" I asked.

"You've got a good memory," he came back. "They're all doing well; really into school and sports."

"And do you still run?"

"Not quite as much as I used to, but I bike to work whenever I can, like this morning. It was a really nice ride."

Knowing both his time and mine were valuable, I changed the subject by asking him to look over my recent blood work from WVCI. As always, I came prepared with my own copies of everything. "I'm most concerned about my real low Ig levels." I sat completely quiet while he examined my last few tests.

"Things look good," he remarked. "Neutrophils are normal, and even though your lymphocytes are still low, they're recovering at a reasonable rate. Ig G is stable, although well below the normal range but I suspect they'll improve. And blood transfusions are a possibility if ever needed. More important than numbers is whether or not you've experienced infections that required antibiotics. Things like bladder infections and pneumonia." He went quiet, awaiting my input.

"I usually pick up a bug during the winter, pretty much like everybody else, most often in the form of a sinus infection, but that's about it. No bladder infections or pneumonia."

"Have you gotten your flu and Shingrix shots yet?"

"Had the second shingles shot recently and the flu shot a couple weeks ago."

"Wish all my patients were as diligent as you are," he complimented me.

"Well, my life just might depend on it. I'd say wanting to stay alive is a pretty strong motivator."

At his direction I climbed up on the exam table and he listened to my heart and lungs and then felt the lymph nodes in my neck, above my clavicle, my groin and spleen.

"Everything is good. Didn't find any swollen nodes and your spleen feels normal in size. I'd say you're doing very good."

I then posed the question about what kind of treatment he'd recommend when my CLL required it again. He, like Sharman, agreed it could be in pill form, probably either Imbruvica or Venetoclax, but also said new infusion drugs might even be more effective. Instead of being on a pill for the rest of my life, short infusion time frames followed by long periods of remission might actually be a better choice.

"There aren't any guarantees, but I'm hopeful your present remission will continue for years because your CLL has shown itself to progress slowly. And by the time your CLL relapses and you need treatment, there's going to be options we don't even know about right now. Maybe even that cure we've all talked about." I heard this before, but liked hearing it again, and again, and again.

"I hope both you and Dr. Sharman will work together to decide my next treatment, when it's needed and what kind is needed," I said in a serious tone, before pausing and adding, "Is that alright?"

"Absolutely," Strother immediately replied. I pretty much knew his answer ahead of time, but wanted to ask anyway.

"How often was Dr. Sharman seeing you and having you do blood work?"

"Every three months because that was the BG clinical trial protocol."

"Well, with your numbers being what they are, I think every six months is called for unless something comes up like night sweats, fatigue or infections. Because your last blood draw was in July and I wouldn't see you until April, that's nine months, I'd like you to go to the lab after our visit. Trina can show the way, okay?"

"Sure," I answered. "And my blood results will be posted on your MYCare Plus website?"

"Yes. And Trina might also call you tomorrow about any flagged results. I'll send her back in. It's good to see you doing so well, Pam."

"You too," I answered. "And thanks." He turned, opened the door, and walked down the hallway; bet he was a long distance runner in high school. Trina arrived and showed me where scheduling was so I could end my visit after having my blood taken by making my next appointment in April. So far, Strother's office ran like clockwork. Now I'd check out their lab and the phlebotomists who poked people for a living.

"Hello, Pam," said a friendly blood drawer who'd already gotten the request via the efficient computer system of the doctor's office. Clearly, my name had already circulated beyond reception to other areas of Oregon Oncology Specialists.

"Might need to warm my left arm up and you might have better luck with a butterfly needle."

"Sounds like you're a veteran," the sweet young lady said and did exactly what I told her.

"Yep, unfortunately I am." She tied an elastic band securely around my upper left arm and gently tapped my veins.

"This one looks real good," she said. And with the quickness and ease of a woman who knew exactly where she wanted to be and exactly what she wanted to do, found a vein and drew my blood and put the important liquid into three tubes. She placed a cotton ball over my tiny poke and then wrapped a thin strip of red gauze around my wound and I was all done.

"That was one of the best pokes I've ever had," I mentioned, not referring to my husband in any way.

"You're very welcome," she said kindly. I was out the door and on my way to scheduling.

"Hello. I'll be with you in just a second," said the stylish lady behind the large computer screen. Recently manicured fingernails, l..o..n..g ones, clicked, clicked, clicked across the keyboard at high speed.

"How may I help you?" she asked politely, looking up from her typing. I handed her the form Dr. Strother had given me, requesting an appointment in six months. She brought her April calendar up and perused it carefully, looking to fulfill my request of another Monday morning time. I always liked being one of the first patients when the day was fresh and so were my health care providers. Also, those appointments were almost always on time.

I remembered my dad telling me about visiting his cardiologist's office and not getting in until 3:30 pm when his appointment was scheduled for 1:00. Dad had taken time off from work and got raked over the coals by his boss at the Oregon Tax Commission for coming back to work about time to get off work. My wonderful and sweet father sent his doctor a bill for the exact amount his boss deducted from his paycheck. For the life of me I can't recall how the whole money situation was resolved, but I do remember Mom telling me that his doctor never again tried to get in a quick nine holes before lunch at Oak Knoll Golf Course on the days dad had appointments.

"Dr. Strother has Monday, April 1st open. You'd have your labs at 7:45 am, followed by your visit at 8:00. How does that sound, Pam?"

"Guess April Fool's Day is as good as any," I joked. She printed my appointment information and I walked out of reception.

The first thing I did after getting home was think about Maryn. My next appointment was scheduled for April; she wouldn't have another April. I wished I could give her some of my remission time so she could share more Christmases, more birthdays, more summers, more everything with her family. Again I wanted life to be fair, but WANT seldom equaled reality.

Some clinical trials work and some don't. I went to the computer and made another donation to Maryn's GoFundMeSite. Doing so really didn't make me feel any better.

Tuesday morning Trina called me bright and early to say my test results had been posted on their website and could be viewed. When I checked them, I was happy to see my IgG levels had gone up 20, but sad to see my IgA falling to 9 and my IgM tanking at <5. Other areas such as platelets, hemoglobin, neutrophils, and lymphocytes were good, but those darn Ig levels were a real worry. I figured Strother's mention of blood infusions just might become more of an on-going conversation. Fortunately, recent scans at OHSU and blood work at the University of Washington both showed no Merkel and that kept the elephant out of the room in comparison to CLL. So good news definitely outweighed the bad.

After Maryn and her family returned from her Make-a-Wish trip to Disney World, the brain cancer spread even more quickly and palliative care at home began. The very dedicated people at Hospice and volunteers at the Portland based children's organization called "Piles of Puppies," helped bring special moments of happiness into her remaining days. Playing with a litter of cute bull mastiff puppies and giving loves to her own dog, Otto, were some of the last things she was able to do.

Maryn died on November 16th, 2018, eight months to the day from her initial diagnosis of brain cancer. Her body was cremated and a Celebration of Life planned later for December 15th. Her mother, Chrissy told all of us, "We do want to celebrate her and not have a solemn, sad affair. She was a fiery, joyous kid, and we want her to go out the same way."

December of 2018, marked three years since I finished my last round of chemotherapy and an added 6 months since I'd consented to take part in a phase II medical experiment combining Bendamustine and Gazyva for the treatment of Chronic Lymphocytic Leukemia. I was in remission and hoped for more of the same.

When leukemia came at me and I was forced to begin treatment for an incurable disease I was terrified, more scared than I'd ever been in my entire life. Yet the trials of the trial had a silver lining beyond killing bad lymphocytes, the hardships I endured taught me important lessons about life and how I wanted to live out my remaining years. Five simple lessons educated me in finding what I wanted most; joy, contentment, and peace of body and mind. All of these cost almost nothing, but each is worth all the money in the world.

What follows is the final section of my book; a look at the five lessons I learned while taking part in a CLL trial which killed the cells that were trying to kill me. These lessons have become part of my every day existence, the essence of what makes me, ME. It's my hope that, MY TRAVELS with the BIG C and a CLINICAL TRIAL that CHANGED my LIFE, will help others reach their own destination and me being a "nobody" in a "somebody" world will not diminish the worth of its message.

LESSONS

LESSON 1

LITTLE IS BIG

Taking part in a clinical trial was an extraordinary experience, a significant detour in my life and my way of looking at it. It changed me. And something I learned was it's the littlest things in life, the commonplace, the minutia of one's existence, that has the greatest capacity to help us in our time of need and bring us the greatest joy.

These small things might be a kiss on the forehead from someone you love, the holding of hands with a daughter who has all grown up, a phone call from a BFF, a homemade card made by a small child, even simply a breath of fresh air out in your own backyard. So, so many tiny things are not tiny at all.

When a clinical trial failed to improve Maryn's life, some small puppies did. They came to her home, and for a brief while she and her family were able to push her cancer aside and let in the love, soft fur, and puppy breath of man's best friend. The small gesture on the part of dedicated volunteers from Piles of Puppies in Portland, Oregon, reaped great reward; they provided a time of happiness during the dying days of a young child and the letting go of a grieving family.

After I sent out my first email to family and friends, telling them about leukemia and my plan to fight it, I received a note from a South High School student who had graduated in the 90's. It read:

Found out you were sick. Want to say thanks for helping me understand that I was worth something when I thought I wasn't. Ready to graduate from college and I owe you that. Hope you feel better soon.

Love, Jason.

I put that short message in the nightstand by my bed and read it every morning during the clinical trial. It helped me feel my life had really meant something to those I'd taught; probably not to David at The Graybar Hotel, but it did to Jason at South Salem. For many years I'd earned high honors in my profession. I was chosen Oregon Alternative Education Teacher of the Year, was the recipient of the Oregon Industries Award, Salem's Crystal Apple Award and South Salem Teacher of the Year Award. Also, I received so many framed certificates, momentos and plaques for educational excellence signed by the likes of CEOs, governors, superintendents and city council members that they overflowed bins in the garage. I even shook the hand of a Vice-President of the United States in honor of my educational feats. None of these things, not a single one of them; however, even came close to making me feel as worthwhile as the five sentences written by an at risk student I taught 25 years ago.

When the hard parts of the trial got harder I kept telling myself that its success would enable me to one day find out if Daenerys Targaryen married Jon Snow and whether the first woman in our country's history would become President of the United States of America. We all need our personal motivators, but those were for the long haul and I needed help for the everyday grinds. They came not as superheroes or famous motivational speakers, but rather as an old horse, a warm blanket and a good poke.

After I experienced the serious reaction to my first chemo treatment and finally settled down and looked out the window, there was a horse doing what horses do- using her long tail as a fly swatter for her back, lowering her head to nibble on grass and gulping water from an old trough. The sheer **sameness** of her actions were a delight to behold, and over time she became a constant companion in my ever changing battle against leukemia. She wasn't simply a pleasant distraction; the small pleasure of watching her lifted me out of my fearful world of cancer and brought me peace. Blondie was my comfort mechanism, like a Binky or favorite stuffed animal is to a child.

During chemotherapy when the drugs entered my body, a sudden and frightening coldness always came over me; not just a simple chill that started and then subsided, but a stone cold chill to the bone. The only way I could escape it was by the warmth of the treatment room blankets stored in nearby containers. They were white, thin and the size a person would use on a twin bed. Most were well worn and frayed around the edges, but miraculously their smell was free of the usual hospital odor. I loved wrapping my whole body in their delicious warmth, tilt back in my brown recliner and close my eyes. The physical comfort of being cocooned during treatment helped tremendously to get through all 15 times Bendamustine and Gazyva was put in my old veins.

I don't have a phobia about needles; heaven's sake, I've been poked well over 100 times. Unfortunately, my veins are in bad shape; they're covered in scar tissue, don't show themselves easily and only my left arm veins are usable. When my body was constantly being assailed by outside sources, I oftentimes got light-headed, dripped sweat and had tumbling blood pressure. A little thing like a good poke with a tiny needle was worth everything, even the down payment for a beach front house in Neskowin. And skilled phlebotomists who pinpointed a vein for good poking and drawing of blood on their first attempt, I am forever thankful and in my humble opinion deserve merit pay and their pictures hung next to Blondie's.

None of these things are spectacular or earth shattering; none are awesome or unbelievable and that's the point. Things in life can be small and appear insignificant; a kiss, a holding of hands, a visiting puppy, a handwritten note, an old horse, a warm blanket, a good poke, and the list goes on and on, but they can also have the power to take on huge importance. When we finally realize that it's the simplest of things that are worth the most and can help us the greatest; that little REALLY is big, then we've taken a giant step toward happiness, peace, and true contentment.

LESSON 2
NATURE CAN HEAL

The world of medicine, its researchers, doctors and nurses, procedures and tests, surgeries and drugs, and especially its vast amount of information about CLL, helped me survive and thrive a clinical trial. Yet during my six months I needed more. I needed something separate and distant from that inside world; something that was part of the world of Mother Nature, a 'mother' who could quiet my worried mind and push the pause button on the sickness of my mental and bodily suffering. The American poet, Walt Whitman explores this as a possible theme in one of his most famous works, "The Learn'd Astronomer", published in 1865, as part of his poetry collection, "Drum Taps."

THE LEARN'D ASTRONOMER

When I heard the learn'd astronomer
When the proof, the figures, were ranged in columns before me,
When I was shown the charts and diagrams, to
add, divide, and measure them,
When I sitting heard the astronomer where he lec-
tured with much applause in the lecture-room,

How soon unaccountable I became tired and sick,

Till Rising and gliding out I wander'd off by myself,

In the mystical moist night-air, and from time to

time, Look'd up in perfect silence at the stars.

Oftentimes during the trial, when fear tightened my chest and I thought I couldn't breathe, I left the lecture room of my home and went outside and tended to my vegetables. I mothered my romaine lettuce, Early Girl tomatoes, snow peas, baby carrots, and Walla Walls sweet onions...and yes, I did talk and sing to them on more than one occasion. (The baby carrots especially liked the song, 'You Are My Sunshine'.) Watching them grow and mature was like watching Karin do the same and, feeling responsible for their well-being, I worked hard to make sure they were safe from harm and that their growth was celebrated. I watered my garden every other morning and pulled weeds whenever their evil heads popped above ground; I staked up branches heavy with mature sweet banana peppers, tomatoes and ripened blueberries, and cured my childrens' illnesses caused by aphids and snails. My garden was my offspring and I felt wonderful caring for someone else .

In October of 2015, the 3rd month of chemo brought about the re-invention of my home's landscape. I needed a project, something purposeful to latch onto, a creative outlet to satisfy my need for changing ugliness into beauty. We'd already spent 25 years bringing back hundreds of pounds of sand from the Oregon Coast and giving birth to Johnsons' Beach, but I longed for a project of much smaller scale. I found that having some grass removed and in its place planting inexpensive ground cover, fulfilled my longing. Now, from every window of our home is a view worth remembering and I don't want to change a thing, especially location.

I love being around water, all kinds of it. During my trial I spent long hours watching the nearby Willamette River flow by Keizer, its current gentle and lazy. All kind of birds, from finches and chickadees, to geese and ducks hunted for food on the river's bank and I breathed more slowly and felt better every time I took in the beauty, both sight and sound, of my feathered friends. Neskowin Beach was the place I gravitated to when the trial really hit rock bottom and I'd been down so long it looked like up to me. Each time I walked her beaches and watched the saltwater waves crash to shore, saw the amazing flat line of the horizon off in the distance and, "in the mystical moist night air," watched in awe at the glory of the sun setting, I felt a spiritual communion with everything, everywhere. Being a part of all that connectedness grabbed the demons in my worried mind and tossed them out and replaced them with the twins of hope and optimism.

Over my lifetime, Mother Nature has gifted me with many an assortment of dogs and cats, some simply neighborhood acquaintances and a few, well loved household pets. My canine and feline pals have come in all shapes and sizes, short-haired and long-haired, young and old, excited and calm; you name it, it's owned me. Charlie, my last pet, was that most unique part of nature who sensed my needs and offered his curative powers generously, expecting nothing in return except my lap and a little affection. Every time I stroked his fur and scratched under his chin, I relaxed, completely relaxed. As one, my mind and body went to a quiet place and my sweet black and white kitty purred along as my beloved traveling companion.

The healing power of nature is strong and comes in all forms for the needs of all kinds of patients. In their own special way, each of mine built sturdy bridges over the troubled waters of my trial against leukemia.

LESSON 3

LEARN THE UNKNOWN

During my clinical trial, I often went low instead of high and worried about running out of time to learn what I wanted to know. Some people decide to take up sky-diving to know what skills are needed to jump out of a plane thousands of feet up in the air and float down to the ground with a parachute. Some people, my husband included prior to becoming a grandfather, decide they want to know about man-eating sharks so they get inside a shark cage and scan the surrounding waters. I'm not like this; it's simply not in my nature. I choose less hazardous ways to make the joy of the unknown, known.

One of the first books I schooled myself with during my clinical trial was THE EMERALD MILE by Kevin Fedarko. It tells the story of the fastest boat ride down the entire length of the Colorado River and through the Grand Canyon during the massive flood of 1983. Its exciting narrative made it hard to put down and with small dosages of geographical information, my longing to learn about the canyon's formation were answered. If I couldn't one day visit it in person, whether because I didn't have the funds or health to travel, I could still "see" it and experience the joy of its wonders. My mental trip to the canyon was grand and glorious.

As a lover of history and great admirer of fascinating people, during my 6 month part time job I finally read well documented and fact-based accounts of Cleopatra, Nefertiti, Madame Curie and King Tutankhamen. I escaped into their world and left the trials of mine. Learning about such people, I recaptured the childish delight of learning new things for the **very first time**. And when I shared what I learned, John was always ready to listen and ask me questions. Learning became a two- way street which made turning the unknown into the known even more thrilling and satisfying.

After having joined Ancestry.com long before the clinical trial, I found out my great, great, grandfather, Joseph Pillett (no 'e' on the end) had, as a young private, been part of the Union's 9th Regiment, Illinois Cavalry during the Civil War. I'd always wanted to know more about this time in our nation's history, especially about the Confederacy and life in the South, both then and now. In many ways our country still didn't seem to be over the Civil War and I yearned to know why. CONFEDERATES in the ATTIC, by Tony Horwitz helped me understand many of the reasons.

I'm not a religious person; I don't look to the Bible for answers to the unknown, rather I turn to science. For decades I'd had a desire to comprehend more about our planet and the universe beyond. Questions plagued me...How was Mother Earth created? What exactly is a black hole? Is time travel truly a possibility and not a fantasy of science fiction? During my trial I felt the over-powering need to investigate these burning questions. If my traveling days were numbered, it was pretty stupid to postpone such fires anymore. Fortunately, I found Stephen Hawkings's New York Times bestseller, THE UNIVERSE in a NUTSHELL, where even my sometimes slow chemo brain could understand what he was saying. After reading each page slowly and carefully, just like the consent form for my clinical trial, contentment in its knowledge far better exceeded ignorance in its bliss.

And it wasn't just books that were my educators and made the unknown, known during the trial, it was also award winning documentaries on television. Two of them were especially amazing, yet heart-wrenching. One was CRIES from SYRIA which examined the children who were so violently affected by their country's conflict, and the other, TROPHY, an analysis of the big game hunting issue and the need for it at the price of sacrificing innocent and majestic animals. No longer ignorant of these issues, I felt empowered to help improve the situations. During my trial when sometimes I just tried to "hang on," I came alive to change things for the better.

All people seek to know the unknown; it's part of being human. What differs between us is the things we want to learn and the way in which we want to learn them. Some people yell, "Geronimo," which by the way is racist, as they jump out of an airplane to better understand skydiving, while other people, like me, read books and watch TV to go from not knowing to knowing. There's a whole lot of unknowns out there, and being in the dark about things is just that, "darkness." Turn on the light; it will make you feel better and at the same time life will take on a richer abundance. And by the way, the best part of it... maybe old dogs can't learn new tricks, but no person is ever too old to learn something new. Everyone who does is the better for it.

LESSON 4

KEEP ON MOVING

Sir Isaac Newton proposed not only the theory of gravity, but the law of inertia in 1687, when he said; "A body at rest tends to remain at rest. A body in motion tends to stay in motion." This pretty well describes my earliest days of the trial, when all I did was Idaho russet myself on a couch in front of the TV set and watched DVD's of old series like MARY TYLER MOORE, BOB NEWHART, and even I SPY until I couldn't take it anymore. I was a pathetic blob and felt like one too. Lucky for me, I got my shit together and hauled myself from the cushions and started moving and stayed moving for the rest of the clinical trial. It was one of the best moves I ever made.

Walking was my main type of exercise; strolls around our neighborhood, taking in the fresh air at Bush Park, strides with John at Riverfront and River Road parks, pleasant ambles at Minto Island and of course, amazing treks across the smooth sands of Neskowin. Walking, like other forms of exercise and physical activity, produce endorphins, those wonderful hormones secreted within the brain and nervous system which play a vital role in a person's overall well-being by warding off pain and perpetuating pleasure. Every single time I walked, I felt better, no matter the walk's location, pace, or number of steps.

One of the perks of reaching Medicare age is I have a $20.00 per month Silver and Fit membership at our local athletic club, The Courthouse. During the trial, and especially while undergoing chemo, swimming afforded me a way to keep on moving that was low impact and much easier on my aging body. I swam inside, out of the sun, and on the advice of my doctors, avoided all hot tubs. I remembered those in the medical profession describing such tubs as, "places teaming with bacteria." And I figured such bacteria desired nothing more than finding a willing host such as me to suddenly kick into overdrive and make people with CLL, very, very sick.

Walking and swimming were great in the sense they got me moving and feeling better, but I was especially glad to have tennis, no matter how little or how lot. Not only did the sport steer me toward normalcy again, it made me feel younger. All my team of doctors, nurses, technicians, and phlebotomists were in their 40's or close to it, and in their company, I felt like a relic. Tennis took me to my female pals, a tribe of baby boomers who remembered phones having party lines, and GP's who made house calls. My favorite sport during the trial also provided me with a much needed cardio-workout, not so demanding I'd fall over with exhaustion, but something that pushed me, got my heart pounding and my body sweating. I always came home from the courts dog tired but happy and ready to return as soon as we could get another foursome together.

I kept on moving throughout the trial as much and as often as possible. Some days it was easy to put on my bathing suit and swim laps in the warm pool or take an evening walk through the neighborhood and "stare in perfect silence at the stars," or meet up with Donna for a tennis match. Other days though, it was really tough to make myself get out of the house and MOVE. Each time I succeeded in doing so, I reaped huge benefits. I was happier, my mind was quieter, and I felt better about myself and my ability to deal with cancer.

LESSON 5
HELP OTHERS

In the midst of my clinical trial, two little kids wanted to help the animals at the Willamette Valley Humane Society, the place from which they'd gotten their own beloved dog, Wilson and cats, Rainman and Boots. We'd heard the non-profit was in desperate straits. They were terribly overcrowded and quickly running out of food and necessary bedding, and there was the chance some 'hard to adopt' animals might have to be put down. Syd and Aiden sounded the alarm to me and John when they saw the story on TV and the four of us put our heads together. The result was our first Summit Avenue Art Fair at their West Salem home.

It wasn't a huge affair lasting days, but it was huge in the sense of teaching us how wonderful life is when help is offered without any selfish expectation of return. ALL proceeds went to the Humane Society; no one got paid for their long hours of work; no one got reimbursed for their craft supplies and no one got a credit on their tax returns. Helping others for the **right** reason was **really** helping others. The only thing we "got" was the desire to do the fair again, which we did another summer.

I had serious reservations about putting my name on the Clinical Trial Consent Form, but the trial was based on the most current medical knowledge available in 2015, and my doctor was an expert in CLL so I signed it. Then along came August when my reaction to Allopurinal was so bad I almost went into sepsis, and then September followed with a blood clot lodged next to my port with the possibility of it traveling to my lungs. Risks of the trial were no longer just words on a document, they were reality, and that reality could be my own death. Such an awakening allowed me to see the clinical trial from a whole different point of view, not one of simply helping me, but of helping others who would survive my participation. Should I die because of it, the reasons why could help others avoid my same end. Maybe doctors could learn to change the dosages of Bendamustine and Gazyva, maybe the frequency or duration of treatments could be altered, maybe better ways to mitigate side-effects could be established and the lessons learned go on and on. Never before in my entire life had I been given the opportunity to perform what I viewed as a noble act, the loss of my life so that others might live. Most people are not given this kind of opportunity, but all of us can and should make our existence one of helping those in need.

During my clinical trial I learned about Maryn's cancer and donated all I could to her GoFundMe site, wishing every single day I was filthy rich and able to pay all her costs, anonymously. But sadly I didn't have a lot of money and still don't; however, one thing I did have instead of the big bucks, was TIME. So when Maryn's mom sent out a message asking for help, I responded immediately. She needed someone to get groceries for a large gathering at a coastal retreat provided free of charge for families of children with terminal illnesses. Chrissy needed the gift of someone's time, that most precious of commodities, and I was honored to give it. If I couldn't give Maryn the outcome of my clinical trial, I could certainly give her mother my time so she didn't use her's away from her dying daughter.

Far too many of us travel through life thinking only of ourselves, but if our lives are to have true meaning, to be successful on any scale, grand or otherwise, then helping others must be our goal. I know I got through treatment, not because I was Superwoman from Keizer, but because I was helped every step of the way by those around me. A poem by Ralph Waldo Emerson, whose work may rightly be attributed to an earlier piece by Bessie Anderson Stanley, sums up what I believe is the most important lesson I learned during my clinical trial and my most important reason for living.

WHAT IS SUCCESS?

To laugh often and much; to win the respect
of intelligent people and the affection of children;
to earn the appreciation of honest critics and endure the betrayal of false friends;
to appreciate the beauty; to find the best in others;
to leave the world a bit better,
whether by a healthy child, a garden patch or a redeemed social condition;
to know even one life has breathed easier because you have lived.
This is to have succeeded!

I was taught five enduring lessons about life during my clinical trial for Chronic Lymphocytic Leukemia, and they appeared to me during times of reflection, pain and pleasure. The unique way they co-mingled in my consciousness and became one over-riding belief, surprised me. All the lessons are connected to the first, Little Is Big. A vegetable garden can quiet a troubled mind, a book can change ignorance into knowledge, moving can improve one's health, and by the simple act of helping others we can add meaning to our existence. The trial not only saved my life; it was the best teacher I ever had.

POSTSCRIPT

I WROTE THIS BOOK during the pandemic of 2020, 4 years after the completion of my 6 month clinical trial and 2 years after finishing all my follow-up visits. It took that much time to distance myself enough so I was able to <u>remember</u> events without the turmoil of <u>reliving</u> them. And it was during those troubled times of social-distancing, mask wearing and hand washing that I received a call from California agent Paul S. Levine encouraging me to self-publish.

I knew I had no name recognition and no previous best sellers so the chance of getting a large publishing firm like Random House or Simon & Schuster to take me on was less than one in a million. Not liking those odds at all, I set two goals for myself; follow Mr. Levine's advice and of course, not get covid-19 because without the second, there would never be a first.

As I wrote MY TRAVELS with the BIG C, I began to take notice of the many comparisons between my disease and the trial I underwent, and the disease of coronavirus and the trials taking place all over the world. Life is like that, parallels often occur without our consciously making them.

My journey with Chronic Lymphocytic Leukemia began in 2009, with its deadly diagnosis and my travels continue today with my remission. I now know Daenerys Targaryen didn't wed John Snow; instead, she was killed by him. Great stories always seem to have twists at the end. I hope my twist is a remission that is one for the record books.

ACKNOWLEDGEMENTS

....

Self-publishing a book has been a huge undertaking, one that I could never have accomplished without the help, expertise and encouragement of others. The following deserve special acknowledgement and my sincere gratitude.

To my manuscript readers; Donna Hirt, Susan Lavin and Sydney Moneke, thank you for generously giving your time so this book could become a reality.

To my skilled copy-editor, Kim Miller, endless thanks for all you did to improve my writing and for being my "sister" in the family of those who have survived breast cancer.

To those at Gorham Printing, thank you for your skillful knowledge of book production and devotion to helping authors. A special shout out to Candacc and Jennifer, and my book designer, Kathy. They all assisted me in countless ways.

To Lewis Media Group in Keizer, Oregon, and especially my talented web-designers, Michael Nolan and Jennifer Lewis, I can't thank you enough for all your hard work.

To local author Kris Lockard, thank you very much for your self-publishing tips and for your excellent recommendation of Gorham Printing.

To doctors, Jeff Sharman and John Strother, and readers, Donna and Susan, sincere thanks for the kind comments you provided for MY TRAVELS with the BIG C. I greatly appreciate you doing so.

To Paul Hirt, thank you for your willingness to share your skilled computer and technical assistance.

Finally, to a very special horse, Blondie, and her wonderful owner, Julie Beckett, thank you in more ways than you will ever know.